ELEPHANT IN THE CLASSROOM

The story of a troubled 8th-grader,
his dog, and a family secret

BY

DARIN ELLIOTT

TMI Publishing, Providence, RI
www.tmipublishing.com

TMI

Elephant in the Classroom

ISBN: 978-1-938371-30-1
TMI Publishing, Providence, RI

www.facebook.com/DarinElliott

TMI Publishing
61 Doyle Avenue
Providence, RI 02906
www.tmipublishing.com

Also by Darin Elliott
(with Alison Leslie Gold)

Elephant in the Livingroom

CASSANDRA'S PROLOGUE

It's been awhile, and I've been through some freaky stuff, but it's me again. 'Who ME?' you may ask. Good question. And a complicated one.

My name is now Cassandra. I know, I know, it was last Cuddles. Well, let me first explain that I was only named Cuddles because the family at the gas station where I was hanging out allowed their 3-year-old toddler to name me. WARNING: It is not wise to let a small child name your pet, especially when that pet has to live with the name for life! That's how you get dogs named Christmas and cats named Poo-poo and goldfish named Spongebob.

But me, I've had FIVE names in my short canine life, six if you consider 'Hey doggie', which I get whenever I am homeless. How would you like it if every once in awhile somebody changed your name? Just like that, somebody said, 'Hey, you're not Bobby anymore, starting today you're Leroy'!

Okay, this would almost never happen to a human. True, sometimes you guys change your own names, like when Stefani Angelina Germanotta became a pop star and changed hers to Lady Gaga. Or if you go to India as Thomas, do some yoga stuff and get all weird, then come back calling yourself Krishnababa.

But we dogs, when we lose our masters and get a new one, we are usually given a new name, like it or not. My original name with my first family was--gosh, it's still so embarrassing to admit -- Bobolina. Then I got lost on a mountaintop and later ended up with a nice family whose daughter named me Beckett after a dead Irish writer she liked. Then I got abandoned accidentally by her drunk dad, was taken to a shelter and eventually chosen to be a Care Dog in a Senior Center where they called me Jasmine after some smelly flower. I ran away from there and lived for months behind a gas station where it became Cuddles, until eventually a family drove in and took pity on my Extreme Cuteness and then brought me home and named me Cassandra, which I really don't mind, even when they shorten it to Cassia (or 'Cass!' when I am really bad, which, as you can imagine, barely happens.)

I have been with my new family for months, but am still getting used to my latest name, which was actually given to me by the youngest member, Zachary. He is nearly 13 years old and gives me the most attention (there are reasons for this, but we'll get to it later). He has an older sister named Tristan who is 15 and paints pictures a lot and wanted to name me Rembrandt or Caravaggio. How goofy is that? I am quite happy with the name Cassandra, especially when *I* recently discovered that it's the name of a Greek princess! *Zach* looked it up on-line at *Wiki…Wiki….Wiki*-something.

But it is still rather confusing when *I* hear my new name—sometimes *I* turn and wonder 'who the heck is Cassandra?' and then realize it's me! On top of that *I* am in a different home where there are new orders and odors. And trials! Like when *I* was first brought to their house and they set up a dog bed in the laundry room, but have you ever tried sleeping next to a washing machine when it's spinning clothes at 1,200 rotations a minute? BANG! THUMP! BANG! THUMP! *I* was getting headaches (yes, we dogs get them too) and having nightmares (ditto). But one day *Zachary* was home from school with a flu thingy (though secretly he told me he was faking it to avoid trouble in class), and he let me come up on his bed with him while he watched old repeats of 'The X-Files'. (*I* admit that *I* had to close my eyes at the creepy parts!) That went on for three days and by the end his parents accepted it, and now—YES!—*I* get to sleep all night on the end of *Zach's* 'Star Wars' quilt or Tristan's fuzzy tiger-stripe bed cover.

Their parents, Mark and Barbara Klossner, have been very patient with me, especially since *I'm* their first dog and have only one-and-a-half ears (more on that later). *I'm* forced to share family cuddles with 2 cats, Vermeer and Dali, and an outdoor tortoise named Lenny, though you can't exactly cuddle something that's covered with a hard shell, so he's no competition for affection. The cats are okay considering they're cats, which we all know are clever, cocky and crabby. They beat each other up a lot, and Dali tries to steal Vermeer's food when they're eating.

Which reminds me—I knew there was a point to all my babbling—cats are not the only creatures to sometimes pick on each other. Zachary is having his own issues with other kids ever since he entered Middle School last year. It's a secret in the Klossner family—Zach hasn't told anybody yet—but I know because he often comes home from school, calls me into his bedroom, and talks to me about problems he's having. A particular problem. One that often makes him cry into his pillow. And even though I now scoot up across his quilt to lick his face, passing R2D2 and Han Solo on the way, it doesn't seem to be enough these past days.

Things are only getting worse, and I'm running out of comforting tactics (and saliva!).

PART ONE

ELEPHANT IGNORED BY
PRETTY MUCH EVERYONE

CHAPTER 1

It's just after 4pm on a weekday and Zachary is bored, lying on the green shag carpet in the living room, a pillow scrunched under his chin as he watches a TV show where some alligators are attacking muskrats on Animal Planet. He closes his eyes at the disgusting parts because he doesn't like seeing violence. Even in films, when a superhero beats up a villain, he often looks the other way. And Boxing and Wrestling, forget it.

His mom arrives home with bags of groceries and plops them on the kitchen counter, drops her keys and cell phone next to them, and peeks around the corner into the living room. "Sorry it took longer than I thought, Zach, but only two cashiers were open and one was that old lady with lilac hair who always pinches your cheeks," she says taking a thin scarf off her head and shaking her short brown hair free.

"Mmm," Zach grunts without looking up from the TV. A 17-foot crocodile named

Chuckles is swishing his tail at another one somewhere in the Nile.

"Hope you were okay alone for a bit," she adds. "And, hey, I told you before: not so close to the TV."

"Mom, that was true when you were a kid with those gross over-sized TVs. It's not the same anymore," Zach replies without taking his eyes off the screen where Chuckles is stomping from the shore up onto dry land, his sharp teeth dripping river water.

"Are you sure?" she asks as she turns back into the kitchen.

"Yeah, I looked it up. Flat screen TVs don't have the same radiation," he answers, then yells back, "And worrying too much about Radiation, by the way, is called Radiophobia. I looked that up, too."

"Mmm." Now it's his mother's turn to grunt.

(Mmm. And that's MY grunt, Cassandra's. I do so because Zachary has developed this weird obsession recently with memorizing phobias, which he looks up on Internet. 'Phobia', he said, is a Greek word for 'fear', like Claustrophobia when you are afraid of small spaces, or Musicophobia if you are afraid of Music. Me, I have Ailurophobia, which is fear of Cats, though mine is not so much Fear as Disgust.)

"So how was school, hon?" Zachary's mom yells from the kitchen while unpacking the groceries. 'Does eighth grade look like it's going to be fun? Any interesting teachers? New friends?"

"It's okay, I guess," Zachary yells back. Then to change the subject quickly says, "Can I have some cheese crackers?"

"Sure, come and get 'em."

Zachary quickly leaps up from the floor and rushes into the kitchen. Cassandra the dog is now revealed, having been hidden while she slept alongside him on the floor, and she, too, quickly jumps up and follows him to the kitchen.

(Of course I do! We're talking Cheese Crackers! Zach always shares his with me and likes to toss one into the air and watch how with my impeccable timing I catch it mid-air every time. I can do it with nuts, cookie bits, and love it most when he tosses popcorn, especially buttered! Once he tried it with olives but I spit them out. BLECH!)

Zachary's sister Tristan arrives home from high school, drops her backpack on a kitchen stool and moans. She has auburn hair down to her shoulders, though she is dying it black these days, and there's a large Hindu OM symbol on the front of her moss green t-shirt with ripped-off sleeves.

"What's that moaning for, hon?" her mother asks.

"People can be such morons," she says sitting on the other stool. "There's this super-weird boy at school, filthy dreads, a snake tattoo on his neck that ends at his ear, and he's like so obnoxious. He told me he thinks Art is a waste of time."

"Oh, honey, don't let it bother you what other kids think," she says putting groceries in the frig. "You do your art because it means something to *you*. That's the point."

"I know," Tristan grumbles as she comes up behind Zachary and grabs the cracker box from him.

"Hey!" he says.

"Hey!" she imitates him. "What, are they *your* crackers?"

"Mom!" Zach whines.

"Tris, be nice. He had them first. You could at least ask."

"Sorry, Zach. Oh, your Holy Highness, may I please have some cheese crackers?"

"Ha, ha, ha. Here!" he says, shoving the box at her, and then stomps out of the room.

"What's up with him?" Tristan asks as she munches on a cracker. Crumbs fall to the floor and Cassandra rushes over and licks them up.

"I don't know. He's getting quieter and quieter. Must be the age."

(It is not 'the age'. There's something else. But I can't tell. I am sworn to secrecy by an oath, hand-to-paw, I made with Zach weeks ago, even if I'm not quite sure what 'oath' means. I'd like to start Googling words I don't know like Zach sometimes does, but dog paws don't work on human keyboards.

A challenge for all those computer techies out there: develop Bark Command for tablets and smart phones!)

CHAPTER 2

The school bell rings at Jarvis Middle School and all of the eighth-graders in Mr. Foley's History class shove their books and notes into their bags and backpacks and quickly leave the room for their next class, bumping into each other. One girl lightly punches another girl's shoulder, and a few pull each others hair on the way out the door.

Zachary, though, stays behind and moves towards the teacher's desk once the other kids have all left.

"Zachary, you have a question?" the balding middle-aged teacher with kind eyes looks up from his desk.

"Yeah, um… I don't understand why if we came over here to America to avoid religious persecution like you said, well, I mean, why did we persecute the Natives that were already here, like, *before* us?"

"Good point. But that's more for a Sociology class than a History one."

"Why's that?" Zachary asks.

"Well, here we just deal with facts, not the 'whys'. Or rather, the 'whys' only in so much as it explains Cause and Affect. We left Europe to have more Freedoms, that's the 'why'. We felt the Natives were in the way of Development, that's another 'why'," Mr. Foley explains.

"Yeah, but... that doesn't explain... "

"Zachary, what you're asking is in the field of Philosophy, or Sociology as I said before. You better get along or you'll be late for your next class."

Zachary leaves slowly, thinking that the teacher really hasn't answered his question at all, and moves carefully along the corridors, quickly across the open quad area, around a bench, past the school flagpole, and into the Boy's Locker Room.

He sneaks over to the row where his assigned locker is, peeks around the corner to see that certain people aren't in the vicinity, then opens his locker and changes quickly into yellow shorts and a navy blue T-shirt with 'Jarvis Middle School' written across the front in matching yellow. He manages to get in and out without a word to or from any of the other boys, which is what he had hoped.

He's alone when he walks out onto the field where they'll be practicing football while most others are in twosomes or small groups. His best friend Leo should be there too, but he's not. His family is away on a short vacation at their mountain cabin near Lake Tahoe, and Zachary is missing him.

Leo and he have been best friends since they were in the same kindergarten class and started playing together on Zachary's jungle gym and the hammock strung between the avocado and lemon tree in his backyard. At age eight they rollerbladed a lot, and at ten they built a treehouse in an old Oak in Leo's backyard with a working trap door and roof that opened up to the sky. They tried a few times over the years to sleep overnight in it, but always got too scared and climbed down in their pajamas, hurrying across the dewy back lawn into Leo's house and sleeping in his bedroom.

Now at age twelve (actually, Leo just turned thirteen, and Zach's soon to follow) they are into blowing things up with firecrackers left over from Fourth of July. Leo started it by putting an empty tin can over one, which sent it flying up high like a rocket then crashing down with a loud metallic THUD. That gave Zachary the idea to put some dirt on top of the can and increase the blast effect as dirt went flying, and that then gave Leo the idea to put an old stuffed animal on top of the can and send it flying too, which eventually became only a stuffed animal and no tin can, which didn't send it flying, but blasted it into pieces of fluff.

(*Let me state here for the record, because I was there, that they did NOT use any stuffed dogs, but rather, a small stuffed dinosaur and then a stuffed cat, which, if you ask me, was rather appropriate.*)

Zachary smiles remembering the jagged tail of a stuffed dinosaur that landed near his feet as he crosses the tennis courts to join his classmates and the P.E. teacher, Mr. Parnell, out on the field. God, he wishes Leo was there. Without him, this was going to be worse than usual.

He approaches the other boys, almost all of which are taller than him. Or at least bulkier—Zachary is slim and gawky, his chestnut hair misbehaving more than usual these days. Because he was born late in October, his parents had to decide whether to enroll him in Kindergarten at age 4, where he'd be younger than most, or when he was nearly 6, where he'd be much older. He seemed ready during his fourth year, so he was always younger than nearly all his classmates by at least a few months.

"Let's see. Who should be the captains to-day?" Mr. Parnell says as he looks over the twenty or so boys.

Zachary winces. He knows exactly who will be chosen, because they always are.

"Padilla and Hirsh," the teacher announces.

Joe Padilla and Steve Hirsh. The two toughest boys in the class, and nearly the whole eighth grade. They move up next to the teacher and began one by one to pick the boys they want on their team, starting, of course, with their friends, and ending with…

Zachary drops his head.

'God, not again,' he mumbles to himself.

CHAPTER 3

On his bike ride home from school, Zachary goes a little out of his way to pass Leo's house a few blocks from his, hoping to see a Burgundy SUV in the driveway which would mean they were back from the cabin. The driveway is empty except for a scuffed-up black plastic trashcan.

Heading on home, he arrives just as his father pulls up in an orange Karmann Ghia, all rounded fenders and small and cute, like a toy car. And old.

"Ancient! Like from the '70's or something!" Leo once remarked.

Zachary and his dad ride into the driveway at the same time, and after Zach drops his bike on the side of the garage, they meet on the curvy brick walkway up to the front door.

"Hey, Zach. Home a bit late. School going okay?"

"Mm," Zachary replies. Then to change the subject, "And you? What are you working on now?"

Zachary's dad, Mark, tall and slim with bushy brown hair, works in Script Development at one of the film studios in Culver City, quite a drive away from their small suburban town near the ocean, but one he makes only once or twice a week, for he mostly works at home. He often tells the family about the film scripts he's working on, and even more interesting to Zachary are the bad ones he's rejected.

"Well, I read one today about an alien race that crashes their UFO near a farmhouse in the mid-west and stays with a family disguised as traveling gypsies until one of them cuts his finger on a steak knife and bleeds yellow goo at the dinner table."

Zachary slaps his palm to his forehead.

"Yeah, I did the same thing after I read it," his dad says.

"And let me guess," Zach says as they reach the front door, "the movie ends with the military being called in and a big battle at the end."

'Almost. It's a SWAT team first, then the military. But, yeah, there's a big battle at the end, sure."

"BORING!" Zachary replies as he opens the front door.

"Tell me about it," his dad says as they walk into the living room. Tristan is already back from school and slumped into the couch reading a book on Impressionist Painters, the two cats Vermeer and Dali stretched out on either side of her, their soft bellies exposed, and Dali's tail swishes lightly as she pets him.

"Hey, Tris. Where's your mom?" Mr. Klossner asks.

"Dunno," she replies without looking up from the pages. "But did you know that the painter Van Gogh cut off his own ear, was put in a psycho ward, and shot himself?"

"Yes, honey, we all know that," her father replies as he wriggles his small black backpack off and drops it on the ground.

"But why, Dad? His paintings are so cool."

"Not a happy camper, Tris. You know many artists are rather… um… melancholy."

"Am I melancholy?" she asks.

"You're psycho," Zachary butts in.

"Zach, not nice," his dad says. "No, Tris, you are not melancholy", and he and Zach head on into the kitchen around the corner.

"Dad, what's Melon Calling mean?" Zachary whispers once out of earshot of his sister.

"Mel-an-chol-y. One word, Zach. It means… sort of sad and pensive," his dad whispers back, then loudly, "Hey, Hon! I'm home. *We're* home. Got Zach with me."

Barbara Klossner appears out of the laundry room with a green plastic basket of clothes just out of the dryer, kisses her husband on the mouth, bends down and kisses Zachary on the forehead, then drops the basket on the kitchen table and begins folding the clothes into four piles for each member of the family. Holding up a pair of 'Transformer' underpants she asks Zachary, "Still fit you?"

"Not really," he answers. "They pull at the crack in my butt."

Mr. and Mrs. Klossner smile at each other, and she tosses the underpants through the air at the large trash bin by the frig. They just barely make it in, one bit slung out over the edge.

"Ten points!" Zachary announces.

Mr. Klossner leaves the room and heads upstairs for a shower, and Zachary drops his backpack on a stool at the counter and sits at another, twisting around towards his mother.

"Mom, am I melongolly?"

"I'm sorry, what, Zach? Are you… ?

"Melongolly. Tris said that some famous painter was, and Dad said it means sad and pensive."

"Oh, *melancholy*. No, good lord, you're not melancholy, honey. Why would you think such a thing?" She stops folding clothes and looks at him.

"I don't know. I don't know what I am. Sometimes I think I can be melangolly."

"MelanCHOLY."

"… that."

"Zach, something bothering you?" she asks. "Is eighth grade too hard? Got some lousy teacher or something?"

Just as he's ready to say something, she picks up a t-shirt from the basket to fold and shows it to him, smiling. It says 'Granny's Favorite Grandson' in faded letters across the front.

"Oh, god, remember when grandma gave you this? Eleventh birthday, I think. How come I never see you wear it? I mean, I can't blame you," and she starts to fold it.

"I only wear it as pajamas to bed. Never outside. I think it'd be even worse if I was caught wearing that thing!" he says.

"Even worse than what?" she asks as she continues folding other bits of clothes.

"Nothing. You know, just… " and he gets up and goes to the cookie jar.

"Are there any more of the snickerdoodles you made?"

"Not now, hon. It's too close to dinner. You got home a bit later the usual. Why's that?"

Zachary turns and leaves the kitchen quickly.

"Nothing. Just school stuff."

(He wouldn't say, but this afternoon is one of those times when he searches for me and calls me up to his bedroom and closes the door. Then we lay on the bed and he tells me some not-so-nice stuff that happened at school during P.E. I'm okay with his confessions, but it would have been better with snickerdoodles!)

CHAPTER 4

Finally the weekend arrives, and finally so does Leo.

Saturday morning after a pancake breakfast--

(from which I got many hunks passed under the table soaked in maple syrup! I think Zach's really starting to like me lots!)

--Zachary jumps on his bicycle and rides over to Leo's to spend the day.

Leo is wearing a new T-shirt that says 'Like The Lake--Lake Tahoe' and the color, crimson red, contrasts with his black hair, which he now wears down to his shoulders but keeps talking about chopping off into a buzz-cut like one of the young pop singers he likes. He is five months older than Zachary, but shorter and chubbier, and there's a slight twinkle in his dark eyes.

They linger the whole rest of the morning in Leo's bedroom playing video games as if they hadn't been apart for a week and a half —Ultimate Ninja Storm 4, which Leo's bet-

ter at, and Assassin's Creed, where Zach's better at the jumping-across-roofs bit, but avoids
beating up on people like you're supposed to
in the game.

Bored, Leo drops his game pad and then
shows Zachary the new keychain he picked
up on vacation—it's the Batman logo of black
wings—and they toss it back and forth at each
other until it hits Leo on the nose and he fakes
screaming in pain, then laughs.

There are posters on Leo's walls from all
three recent Batman movies, and also one from
'Ironman 3' and 'The Avengers'. Next to those
is a poster of an airplane cockpit centered over
his study desk, because Leo wants to be an airline pilot when he grows up. All around the
room there are models of airplanes that he
made—on his desk, in a wall of bookshelves,
a few hanging from the ceiling with clear fishing line so they appear to be flying. Even both
quilts on the bunk bed have airplanes on them,
and soon the two boys are climbing up on the
top bunk and one by one sliding off, hanging
almost mid-air before crashing to the floor, or
curling up their bodies and landing onto the
lower bunk, the quilt and pillow now a rum-
pled-up tangle.

There is a bunk bed in Leo's room because he used to share it with his older brother, Gordon. But a few years ago he got very ill with a flu (at least that's what Leo's parents told him) and died at age 13, just about the age Leo and Zachary are now. He doesn't talk about his brother much, and Zachary is careful not to bring it up, because he knows Leo misses him too much and it makes him sad to remember.

Among some airplane models high up on a shelf, there is a trophy that Gordon had won in an Archery Competition at day camp his last summer alive.

That's all that is left in the room to show he ever existed. Leo's mom, Mrs. Werner, removed all his things a few days after he died, but allowed Leo to keep the trophy after he begged her.

"Leo, Zach. Lunch!" Mrs. Werner calls from far away in the house, just as Leo is attempting to slide off the upper bunk face down, groaning the whole way down.

Zachary climbs down the bunk bed ladder, pulls Leo down by his knees until he lands all scrunched up on the floor, and runs out of the room, with Leo quickly after him.

After finishing the toasted cheese sandwiches and apple slices and glasses of lemonade that Leo's mom made them--

(Wait! Wait! Back up! Did I hear toasted sandwiches? Cheese? Toasted Cheese? Gooey and slimy and warm and all buttery and crunchy? Zach, pal! How could you leave me at home with fake-meat kibble and a bowl of water with fur floating on top? I thought we were best pals now, buddies, soul-mates. Even if I am a dog and you are a boy, I bet in our past life I was the kid and you were a squirrel or something, and I fed you nuts and seeds and bits of MY toasted cheese sandwich! Really, dude! Bad Karma!)

--Zachary and Leo hop on their bicycles and head towards a part of town away from their school and far from where most of the other students live. It's a hilly area full of plum orchards and an old dried-up creek, and they often go there to ride up and down on the dirt trails. There nobody knows them, so nobody can bother them. It's their retreat from the increasing hassles of Monday-to-Friday at school.

As they careen up and down the trails, Zachary notices that his bike is really getting too small for him, or he too big for it, and mentions it to Leo.

"Yeah, I noticed it, too," Leo says when Zachary points it out at the top of a steep dirt mound, wiping sweat from his forehead.

"See how my legs are all crammed, like they can't stretch out enough anymore?" Zachary shows him.

"Birthday coming soon, dude! After that, Christmas!" Leo smiles, then makes a strong pedal up and over the mound tearing down the squiggly hill path. Zachary follows right behind him.

"YEEEOOHH," they screech as they race down the hill, loose dirt flying about everywhere.

When they arrive back to Leo's house in the late afternoon, covered in red soil, Mrs. Werner insists they both take a shower —"And a long one! Or no dinner!"

The boys don't whine too much after she tells them that the dinner awaiting them is chili beans with her famous Mexican cornbread. One by one they have a shower and put back on their same clothes after shaking off most of the red dirt so Mrs. Werner won't notice.

After the meal, Leo asks if Zachary can sleep over, so Mrs. Werner calls Zachary's parents, gets Mr. Klossner, who agrees, and they settle down to a bowl of popcorn and a DVD of "Man Of Steel" with Mr. and Mrs. Werner and their small white poodle Gwendolyn.

(And I'm stuck at home with more kibble for dinner and a dorky sit-com after the news. At least Tristan's taking an interest in seeing that my cuddle-needs are met, as I'm on her lap on the couch, those two beastly cats nowhere to be seen. And though I understand why Zach enjoys the sleepovers at Leo's, it's beyond me how any sane family can actually choose a poodle as their pet—they're yappy, dippy, and quite frankly, an embarrassment to our species. Nothing noble about poodles. And that's not just MY opinion. It's the shared opinion of every non-poodle dog on the planet. Trust me.)

When the DVD ends, Mr. Werner shakes his wife who's dozed off towards the climactic battle at the end of the film and as she's getting up she asks the boys if they enjoyed it.

"Not really," Leo grumbles. "Pretty lame, actually."

"Zach?" she then says while picking up empty popcorn bowls and greasy napkins.

"Same," Zach answers. "Superman's supposed to be, like, Mr. Nerd and then Mr. Cool. That guy was just like all melancholy."

"Melancholy. Hmm, pretty big word," she responds.

"I learned it the other day," Zach says proudly. Leo punches his shoulder.

"You kids are observant. It *was* rather dull," Mr. Werner adds. "So dull that I'm off to bed this minute. Leo, can you guys shut everything off okay? Doors are locked already. Oh, and there's some leftover cornbread if you're hungry."

"Got it, Dad," Leo replies, getting up to switch off the TV and DVD player. And as soon as his parents leave the room, the two boys turn and rush to the kitchen.

"Cornbread and...let's see...ketchup or peanut butter?" Leo asks, using a spatula to cut and serve huge hunks of bread onto two plates.

"Peanut butter for me," Zachary says, and spreads a huge plop on the top of his piece while Leo plops ketchup on his.

"Look," he says smearing some ketchup purposely on his lips as he takes his first bite, then rolling his eyes back and moaning like a zombie, "Arrrrgh."

Zachary giggles and takes a big bite from his, the peanut butter sticking to the roof of his mouth.

"Subermon wa vawy supid, huh? Na goo fim," Zachary mumbles.

"Huh? That makes no sense, dude."

Zachary takes his finger and scrapes the peanut butter off the roof of his mouth. A big glob dangles on his fingertip.

"I said it was a stupid film. No good," and he licks his fingertip slowly.

"Yeah, really. Who makes these bad films? I mean, why spend all the money? They could have done it, like, really good. But no: Boring!"

"My dad says the studios are run by corporations now and all the big guys at the top know nothing about films. 'It's all about money', he says. Besides, that was a reboot, ya know."

"Yeah, but the Batman reboots were way cool. 'Dark Knight' was like super-cool. And Batman's way better at getting the bad guys."

"Wish I could be like him and stop the bad guys."

"What bad guys, Zach?"

"You know…."

"Oh. Them. Yeah, I wish."

Leo then goes to the frig and opens the door and inspects inside, calling out—

"Orange juice, apple, sparkling water, chocolate milk, or this herb tea thing my mom makes? It's not too awful."

"Apple, please," Zach replies. "Ooh, maybe apple-orange mix."

"How about all of them together?"

"Sure."

And they go upstairs to Leo's room with a tall glass each of orange, apple, chocolate milk and herbal tea mix.

"Not bad," Zachary says as they flick on the light and sit on the floor to work on a model airplane that Leo only half finished.

"Could be better," Leo says after a sip. "Maybe we'll add Pepsi too next time."

CHAPTER 5

Monday morning comes too fast for every-body. Mrs. Klossner grabs her grey leather briefcase and rushes out the door without kiss-ing anybody to drive to the University where she teaches two Philosophy courses.

Mr. Klossner is not on such a tight schedule and gets to do much of his work at home on the computer and in phone conferences, so he lingers over a second cup of tea while skim-ming over the day's newspaper at the kitchen table.

(Which was delivered to him by none other than Moi. Slobber-free, I might add. It's just one of the many wonderful things we dogs can do that neither cats nor a tortoise can: fetch the morning paper. Please note if you are considering what species to get for your next pet.)

Tristan passes the arched kitchen doorway on her way out and her father notices.

"Hey, yo! Tris!"

She backs up and peers in the doorway to her dad.

"Can I see it? C'mon... ," he pleads.

Tristan walks over to him while flinging her lime green backpack off and carefully slides out a large piece of paper and lays it on top of the newspaper in front of him. It's a sketch in pastels of Cassandra and looks almost just like her.

"Pretty good, sweetie. You even got the half-ear right," he says patting her back.

(Stop right there! Must she include my damaged ear? Couldn't she take some artistic license and fill in the ear so that I look more...elegant? I thought Art was about idealizing things?? Wouldn't an Idealized Moi have two full ears? I mean, really!

Gosh, I hope she didn't make my snout look too long as well!)

"You're really improving, Tris. Good work," he adds.

'Thanks, Dad. Gotta go or I'll be late," Tristan says as she slips the paper carefully into her backpack and rushes off and out the front door.

Mr. Klossner turns the page to the newspaper and shifts his legs, nudging the dog under the table.

(But do I complain? No. Part of being the family pet is putting up with inconveniences: bad food, being

left alone too much, having to sit through dumb DVDs, stupid cats for siblings, not to mention Lenny the tortoise! Cuddles, walks and endless snacks make up for it, so I restrain from biting his foot off for kicking me under the table.

I raise my head and perk up my one-and-a-half ears when I hear:)

Zachary clambers down the stairs and he, too, passes by the arched doorway to the kitchen without stopping.

"Yo, Zach. No hug Good-bye?" his father calls after him.

('Yo, Zach. No dog-pat Good-bye?' I look up and say to myself.)

Zachary backs up and stands at the open archway.

"Seriously, Dad? You need a hug that bad?"

"Yeah, sure. Course I do. Dads need hugs, too. Besides, you're not even 13 yet. Don't tell me you're too old to hug your old man?"

Zachary walks over to him to offer a quick hug, but his dad's arms around him feel good, and he lingers. They somehow make him feel secure. Safe. When he pulls away, his dad says, "Thanks, bud. That was a nice one."

But instead of leaving, Zachary doesn't move. He just stares at his father, eyes to eyes.

"You're looking good, son. I like that wild chaotic hairstyle on you. And....is that a faint mustache I see coming in?"

Zachary just keeps looking at him in the eyes, as if he's waiting for a good opportunity, the right moment to say something. He wants to, but he just can't bring himself to, and secretly hopes his father will force it out of him. But his dad suddenly notices that one of his son's shoelaces is loose, and bends down to re-tie it for him. When his face comes back up, he notices slight tears in Zachary's eyes.

"Zach, what's up? You can tell me," his father says grabbing his shoulder.

Zachary wipes his eyes with his shirtsleeve and turns to go.

"Nothing, Dad. Love ya....."

"I love you, too, son," Mr. Klossner says, and Zachary disappears out the arched doorway and soon the front door opens and closes and he's gone.

The house is silent, and Mr. Klossner turns to the next page of the newspaper and takes a sip of tea.

Cassia rolls over under the table and shows her belly. She wants a hug, too, but doesn't get one.

(Hey, I can speak for myself, thank you very much.
I roll under the table and show my belly. I want a
hug, too, but don't get one.)

CHAPTER 6

When Zachary arrives at school, he gets off his bike and finds any empty slot in the bike racks near the front of the school (the ones in the back where the tough kids hang out to smoke are too dangerous), unwinds the plastic-covered chain from around his seat post and slides it through the back tire spokes and around the metal poles and locks the two ends together tightly.

When his head comes up he sees Padilla approaching with Johnson, another tough kid, and drops back down pretending that he's still locking his bike. But they've already spotted him and grab the handlebars of his bike and shake it violently as they pass. The front wheel bangs hard against his cheek, and it hurts.

"Mamma's boy!" Padilla calls out, and Zachary cringes.

"What a friggin' dweeb," he hears Johnson snicker as they wander off.

Zachary waits a few minutes more before rising up, then quickly walks off in the opposite direction that they went. Wiping his cheek to check for blood, he notices a few students nearby staring at him, some giggling, as he passes.

After Mathematics, which he's good at but doesn't like much, and after Biology, which he is also good at but actually likes, it's time again for P.E. Cautiously, he makes his way into the boys' locker room, slips between rows of lockers and benches to find Leo already halfway dressed in his sports clothes.

They slide palms together and smile lightly.

"Hey, dude, you've got like a sort of black eye," Leo says as he reaches over to touch it.

"Yeah, it's nothing. Bike bit me," Zachary replies as he turns the combination lock on his locker, opens the door and hangs his grey hoodie up inside.

Blocked by the open door, he can't see what's going on, but hears some kind of ruckus, and Leo's voice, gagged, trailing off. He pulls his head out of his locker to find Leo gone, his locker still open and his sneakers on the floor.

A horrible chill overcomes him, and his heart starts pounding. He takes a breath, then nervously walks to the end of his row of lockers, looks around the corner, sees nothing, and slips into the next row. There he hears a tapping on metal, and the muffled call of his name. Moving down the row, ever closer to the voice of his friend, he finally locates the locker where some other boys have shoved Leo in, and quietly lifts the latch and opens the door. Leo comes out, straightens up, and they look at each other for a second before heading back towards their lockers.

"Love P.E. Just love it..., " Leo smirks, quietly pushing Zachary ahead of him to go faster.

When they reach their lockers, Zachary kicks off his shoes and starts to undo his belt, then suddenly stops, frozen. Leo's almost finished getting into his sports clothes and turns to see his friend standing still staring into the darkness of his locker.

"Zach, c'mon. We'll be late... "

"Why bother? Let's just get outta here. I hate this place."

"Me, too, but...whatda ya mean? Ditch class... ?

'Yeah, c'mon!" Zachary says as he sits and puts his shoes back on.

"But... I... I've never ditched class before..."

"Me either. Let's just get outta here. Quick!"

Leo hurries to get out of his uniform and put his street clothes back on. They slam their lockers shut and sneak out of the locker room.

"Where do we go?" Leo asks as they enter the corridor outside the Gym.

"Does it matter? Anywhere but here!"

CHAPTER 7

Zachary decides not to mention what happened in the locker room when he gets home that afternoon, or that he and Leo cut class and hung out at the wild almond orchards nearby, throwing stones at tree trunks—ten points if you hit one head-on, five if you skimmed a trunk, and one for every leaf that falls from the impact. Zach won 74 to 58, and they left the orchard feeling better, as if distracting themselves from what had happened in the locker room made it almost seem like it hadn't. In any case, they had each other, neither was alone, and they were both silently thankful for that. And if anybody at home asks about the small bruise under his eye, he'll just say that he missed catching a ball in P.E. They'll believe that, knowing he's not very good at sports.

On their way home, weaving their bikes in and out of a line of trees along a dirt trail, Leo suddenly blurts out an odd phrase: "To, Too, and Two."

Zachary's on to Leo's sudden obsession with crazy English, and knows what's coming.

"Think about it," Leo yells over to him. "Three different spellings but all with the same sound. Crazy, no?"

"Never thought about it," Zachary mumbles.

"Huh? Can't hear you!"

"I Said, I Never Really Thought About It."

"Like, you can actually say 'Are you going to room number two? I'M GOING TO TWO, TOO', and it's okay."

"Mm, yeah, I guess that is kinda odd," Zachary says just to be nice, perplexed at Leo's recent obsession with pointing out crazy stuff about the English language.

Mrs. Klossner teaches only one class on Mondays, so she is always home earlier than usual. Zachary arrives to find that she's been baking oatmeal chocolate chip cookies, saving the bowl and wooden spoon for him to lick, and offering him two hot cookies fresh from the oven. He steals a third from the plate, which she notices but says nothing. She's a little worried about him--something's changed since he started the eighth grade, but she cannot put her finger on it, and thinks maybe he is just going through the physical changes of becoming a teenager. But too scared to discuss that either, she simply lets him take a third cookie if that makes him happy for the moment.

On his way up to his bedroom Zachary passes Tristan's room. The door is open wide and he wanders in. He's always gotten along well with his older sister, and takes a seat on her bed after dumping his backpack on her floor.

"You might ask me before you just enter," she says without looking up from the notepad she's writing in.

"Sorry. May I?"

"Yes, you may, Monkey," she says, using a nickname that she's called him since he was four and loved to hang from tree branches, but which she hasn't used recently. Somehow hearing it now comforts him a bit, like his mom's homemade cookies. And he needs all the comforting he can get.

While she continues to write into the pad, he looks around the room—it's been awhile since he's been in there for more than just a quick glance, so he's surprised how different it seems now.

All of the posters of One Direction and Taylor Swift are down, and even the faded one of Mulan that's been over her headboard for years has been replaced. Up now are some of her sketches and paintings, as well as some weird fabric scroll thing with an oriental figure seated in the middle.

"Hey, what's that?" he asks pointing up at the odd hanging. Tristan glances up for a second, then looks back down and continues writing.

"It's called a Tanka. Tibetan Buddhist thingy. Like it?" she says.

"Yeah, it's sorta… weird. But nice weird."

His eyes wander further and notice a quartz crystal hanging on a thread in her window, and a thin stream of smoke rising from a wooden slat on her desk, and suddenly he's aware that there's an odd smell. He likes it, and gets up to wander over and see what it is.

She looks up and notices him reach for the incense box.

"Patchouli. From India."

"Cool."

Just then he hears purring nearby and looks around and sees Vermeer high up on her bookshelves stretched across a row of paperbacks. Two shelves lower is Dali nudged between a statue of some dancing Hindu god and large books on Art History. Dali opens one eye when he notices Zachary watching him, and readjusts himself in his cramped spot.

(That ridiculous posing of the cats reminds me of a recent documentary on TV in which the innate skills of Dogs were compared to that of Cats. Imagine! Like there's any competition! We dogs came out best for Ability to Smell and To Be Trained. And Okay, Cats proved better at some things, like Night Vision (who needs it?) and also The Ability To Jump Up On High Places. (Ditto). That's why those two feline nitwits are hanging off the shelves while I am down here on the floor, wondering why Zach hasn't noticed me yet.)

"Cassia, hey sweetie," Zachary says spotting the dog on the floor and moving down to rub her on the head.

(Ha! He heard my wish!)

"Right," Tristan suddenly says as she pushes the notebook to one side and pats the end of her bed. "Come back here, I need your help."

Zachary moves back to her bed and sits again on the dark blue quilt with green cross-weaving.

"That's new, too," he remarks, his hand moving across the quilt.

"Got it in a Thrift Store. That shade of blue corresponds to your fifth chakra, at the throat—Self-Expression," she explains, grabbing her neck.

"Chalka? What's that?"

'ChakRA, means 'wheel'. In India they believe we have seven energy centers running down our body, each corresponding to the seven colors of the rainbow, red at the base—your butt—and violet at the top of your head."

"Whatever," Zachary mumbles.

"Listen, we have to turn in a portrait tomorrow for Art class and I want to do you." Then noticing the faint black eye, says, "Hey, how'd that happen?"

"Missed a ball in P.E.," he answers. "You know…"

"Oh, well, doesn't matter. I won't put it in your portrait."

"But why me? I mean, what about your friend Alison or something?"

"It has to be a relative, and Mom and Dad can't sit still. I thought of doing Cassia just to make a point about pets being relatives, too, but I already did her when the subject was animals."

(She's done me numerous times, actually. Pencil sketches, charcoal, pastel. She says it's because I sit— well, lie—still for long periods without moving, but I'll

bet it's because I am so adorable. And Adorable, as we all know, makes good art!)

"Okay, I guess… " Zachary finally replies. "But, I mean, what do you want me to do, sit or stand or what?"

"Whatever you feel like," she says getting up and crossing the room to get her pastel pencils and sketch pad. "You're as much a part of it as me."

She notices his nervousness and hesitation.

"Zach, what are you most comfortable doing? Sitting on the bed, on the chair, on the floor, standing up, lying down, what?

"Me….I'm not really comfortable doing anything."

"C'mon, Zach. Don't be that way. You're an okay kid."

"*You* say that…"

'What do you mean?"

"Nothing," Zach replies, then quickly gets up and moves to her desk chair. "I guess I'll sit here like this, okay?"

"Yeah, sure. But you have to stay real still for a while. Unless you want your face a blur, or your nose where your neck is," she jokes, trying to calm him.

They both crack a smile.

"My nose where my neck is? Who'd paint a person's face like that?" he asks.

"Um, HELLO? Haven't you heard of Picasso?" she says as she settles on the bed laying out her pastel pencils so she can see all the colors. "He'd make one face into two, or into half a face, or one eye up and one down…."

"Sounds gross."

"*Is* gross. But he's considered one of the greatest artists of the twentieth century," Tris says as she begins a quick outline of Zachary on the sketch pad.

"By putting one eye up and a nose on the neck…?"

"Believe it or not, yes. Modern Art, dear brother, Modern Art." And she looks up at him then back down to the sketch pad, adding his arms and hands.

"Get this," she says as she continues sketching, "one guy just showed a urinal and said 'This is my art'. And some woman in England took her mattress on the floor with dirty sheets and passed *that* off as art."

"Ew. Double gross!" he says scrunching his nose.

"Hey. You have to stay still."

"Oops. Sorry."

"Her dirty mattress won awards, by the way," Tristan adds.

"Well, I mean, *any*body can do art then," Zachary says trying not to move as he speaks.

"Yep, apparently so."

"Maybe I should try."

"You should, Zach. You might find it helps release some inner stuff. But, um, please, stay still…you need to stop talking or I might give you two mouths!"

Later that evening in bed he thinks about what she said, and tries to doodle on a small notebook he keeps by his bed to write down any dreams he remembers. Recently the dreams are all about being chased, and he often wakes up sweaty and can't get back to sleep, calling Cassia up near his head to cuddle her.

(Indeed he does. I can verify that. In fact, more and more Zach is patting the bed up by his pillow and calling me to come closer to him. I think he really needs me, more than Tris or his parents, or even Leo, so I try to be nearby nowadays. And, hey, free cuddles! I'm not going to refuse!)

"Yuck!" Zachary moans as he rips another page off the notebook. It was a sketch he attempted of Cassia laying at the end of his bed but looks more like half Tyrannosaurus, half loaf of bread.

"Maybe my art should be writing poems," he says to Cassia as he calls her up and rubs her belly. "Except that I don't know how to write poems," which Cassia pretends to care about and licks his hand.

(*It's the best I can offer. Poor kid's a bit troubled these days….*)

"Maybe Haiku……or….Limericks!"

Zachary's mother used to read him Limericks after bedtime stories when he was younger, and he always liked how the phrases sort of bounced. And he really liked that they were silly.

He picks up the notebook again and tries to remember the five-line rhythm of Limericks, and then tries to think of anything that rhymes with the word Barf. But he can only think of Scarf.

Then he tries to rhyme Puke, and comes up with Duke, Fluke, and Nuke as he goes through the alphabet in his head. Oh, and Kook and Spook, he jots down. But it's hard to connect Puking with Nuking, or with a Duke, and he can only get as far as:

'There once was a queasy old duke,

who thought it was way cool to puke.....'

Not able to continue with that one, he rips the page off and writes the word 'Fart' on a new page, and again goes through the alphabet in his head to find all the words that rhyme with it--Art, Bart (as in Simpson), Cart, Dart, Heart, Mart, Part, Smart, Start, and Tart, writing each down, then playing with them to see what would work as a theme.

He persists, forgetting about everything else. (*Except Moi.*)

"If Tris can do art then so can I," he tells himself.

And an hour and many ripped-off pages later he finally comes up with this:

A young boy whose nickname was Bart
would often reply with a fart.
Was the cause a bad belly?
Or did he like being smelly?
Said he, 'Passing wind is my Art'.

He reads it over a few times, smiles, and rolls over, if not tired, at least joyous that he'd succeeded in writing his first poem.

CHAPTER 7½

Hey, it's me, Cassia.

Impressed by Zachary's attempt to express himself through writing, I figured I should attempt the same and tell a bit of my story. So while Zach reads in bed, his parents pay bills at the kitchen table, and Tristan listens to Tibetan Chanting in her headphones, I will take this opportunity to delve deeper into my past and trace my origins. No, not my distant ancestral past— I'm what you humans call a Mongrel or Mutt, but we dogs refer to as a Unique Blend, so my family tree is a mess!—but to my own personal Past.

I mean prior to being Cassandra or Cuddles or Jasmine or Beckett. I mean:

THE PLIGHT OF BOBOLINA

I was born in an animal shelter on the corner of 3rd and Dominga next to a Krispy Kream, so my puppy-hood was dominated by the smell of donuts cooking in hot fat. Other than that, my early days are all a blur of fur.

My first real memory is being bitten on the tail by my slightly-older brother (he came out four minutes be-

*fore me) and my mother yapping at him and then licking
me for comfort. I never trusted that particular brother
after that; out of my four brothers and sisters, he was
the meanest. When I was drinking milk from my mom,
he'd often push me off and I'd have to struggle to find
another spot to drink. I call him Biff in my memoirs
(hopefully to be published soon), but in fact, we had no
names then. The people at the shelter who named my
mom Sparky just called us 'cute' or 'adorable' or 'clever'
or 'tiny' or 'cheeky'. I don't know what they meant by
'cheeky' (I think it's British), but I preferred 'adorable'.
And Adorable I was! Moreso, I might add, than my
brothers and sisters.*

*My original family, that is, the ones who took me
home from the shelter when I was no bigger than a loaf
of bread, were called the Heffernans. I suppose it was
my Extreme Adorableness, or maybe the twinkle in my
eyes and cute runny nose, that made them pick ME and
not one of my siblings.*

*But pick ME they did! And though it was a shock
to NOT be in a cage, and to throw up on that first car
ride home, and then to be passed from kid to kid to kid
to kid to kid (Mrs. Heffernan had given birth to FIVE
kids, just like my mom Sparky!), I couldn't believe my
luck in getting a real home. Not that I knew what 'real
home' meant at that time, for I was only one month old
and knew only pee-poop-play-suckle up to that point.*

But now I had my own bed! Lots and lots of cuddles! Good food! Rags and balls, and orange socks (that I stole from the toddler's room) to play with, and a huge yard to run around in with them.

I started to grow quickly, and I must say, quite ravishing with my cedar-brown fur with vanilla-cream spots, and just a touch of coffee-color highlights. Not to mention my dewy hazelnut eyes that everybody sighed over (especially when I gave them the Extra-Special-Cute Look. You humans fall for that every time, and it always got me LOTS of extra treats over the years!)

Early on they started to take me to a large park and some of the kids would throw sticks or Frisbees for me to chase, until I started chewing off bits of the Frisbees and they stopped bringing them. That's when I learned Lesson #1 As Pet Dog: Don't Piss Off Your Masters. You guys just don't seem to like it when we chew on things that WE prefer to chew on, like chair legs or the car seatbelt or Mr. Heffernan's leather shoes ("Those cost over $100!" he yelled at me, like I knew what THAT meant!). Or when we eat what WE want to eat, like little Suzy's birthday cake before the party, or Mrs. Heffernan's special diet cookies off the counter (those came back up in a jiffy!), or hotdogs straight off the barbeque grill. All of those things got me a swat on my cute little puppy butt and a "Bad Dog!" pronouncement, which made me feel really guilty, so I stopped much of them. (*Confession: I still stole socks from the toddler's floor when nobody was looking, and after a good play with them out back, I'd bury them so nobody found out.*)

So, slowly the Heffernan's were getting to know me and I was getting to know them. Like, what food little Dylan hates and would discreetly drop on the floor under the kitchen table for me: liver, green beans and Swiss chard. Or when it was appropriate to sleep underneath Suzy's covers with her: during thunderstorms or if her older sister Lizbeth stole her doll. Or how many leaks I could make on the living room carpet per week before they'd fling me out back with no dinner: three.

I was fairly happy in every way but one: I still had no proper name. They just called me 'puppy' or 'hey, you', or in the case of the baby Harris, 'boo boo'. Of course he called EVERYTHING Boo-boo or Gee-gee or Uh-uh, which I suppose is normal for a nine-month-old kid, but I was having trouble getting an identity.

Then one day baby Harris started calling me 'Boo-boo' over and over, which became 'Boo-booly', which the eldest kid Nathan extended further to Bobolina, and that somehow stuck. FINALLY! I had a real name.

Second Confession: Although it was better than 'hey, you', I never really liked that name. It seemed more appropriate for a hobbit or some kind of Russian dessert.

Third Confession: They soon started to leave me alone a lot during the day, when the adults went off to work and the kids to their schools and nurseries, which I didn't appreciate, being a needy puppy.

Worse still, Mr. Heffernan started to slap me with a rolled-up newspaper when I yapped at the window at some passing dog/cat/bird/postman, or when I accidently forgot The Dog Rules and chewed on the couch legs or piddled on the green-checked linoleum kitchen floor.

Then things changed drastically one week when all the kids were away at their grandma's and I sort of mistook one of Mr. Heffernan's tangled underpants left on the floor for a play toy and dragged it all over the house and then out into the backyard where I proceeded to gnaw on it until it was in two pieces.

'Play is the highest form of research', that famous human Albert Einstein once said. But Mr. Heffernan apparently hadn't read Einstein, because when he caught me attempting to grab both pieces with my mouth to play tug-of-war with him, he did not seem to be in a playful mood. It was the first time he yelled so loud that it hurt my ears. Then he picked me up quite aggressively, slapped my butt and threw me in the bathroom with the door closed. For hours!

"Bad Bobolina!" he'd yell and bang on the door every once in a while. I just cowered in the corner behind

the toilet, trying to figure out what I did wrong, and wishing that he'd picked my brother Biff from the shelter instead of me....

Uh oh, gotta stop here. I just saw Zach turn off his bedside lamp, so I better quickly go up and take my place alongside him before he falls asleep and No Cuddles!

Sorry, I have my priorities.

PS--To Be Continued.

CHAPTER 8

Zachary and Leo both pull brown paper bags out of their backpacks for lunch. They are sitting amidst a bunch of trees and shrubs out beyond the school quad where nobody can see them. It's a secret place that they discovered a couple weeks ago when the name-calling got so bad in the school cafeteria. This is where they now meet at lunch-break every day.

Before they start eating, Zachary hands Leo a copy of the Limerick he wrote.

While Leo reads the poem, Zachary keeps on the lookout, just in case.

"Wow, good!" Leo says handing the paper to Zachary.

"No, I made that copy for you to keep," he says handing it back. "I'm gonna try to write one Limerick a week."

"What's a Limerick?" Leo asks removing his cheese sandwich from his paper bag. Zachary notices through the clear plastic wrapper that there is a small piece of paper, like a label, on the sandwich.

"What's that?" he asks.

"Mom's trying out new cheeses from around the world, and she wants me to report back on my opinion," Leo answers, then reading the paper, "Gor-gon-zo-la Dolss," he says.

"It's pronounced 'Dole-cha'," Zachary says, reading over Leo's shoulder at the two words written on the paper: 'Gorgonzola Dolce'.

"How do you know?"

"Cuz my dad and I watched this Italian film last month called 'La Dolce Vita'. Means 'The Sweet Life', he said. It was a bit boring, especially because you have to read all the words in English at the bottom of the screen."

Leo takes a slow careful bite.

"Why were all the words at the bottom of the screen? That's weird," Leo remarks through his chewing.

"Italian film, Italian language, so they put the English translation at the bottom so you can understand it," Zachary explains, then takes a bite of his sandwich. He looks over at Leo who is making a face of disgust as he chews.

"So? How is it?" Zachary asks him.

"Um… a bit moldy taste. I think it's gone off."

Leo throws it back in the paper bag and grabs an apple. Zachary feels bad for him and rips his sandwich in two pieces and hands one to Leo.

"Thanks. What is it?"

"The usual. Peanut butter with honey on whole wheat."

Leo takes a bite, then remembers that Zachary never answered his question.

"So you didn't tell me. What's a Limerick?"

"'An Irish form of poetry with humor', Wikipedia says," Zachary answers. Then adds, "And Fear of Poetry is called Metrophobia, by the way."

"Hey, what's with these Phobia things all the time?" Leo asks, enjoying the peanut butter after so many international cheeses.

Zachary lowers his sandwich, staring down at it as he speaks.

"I don't know. Why? Do you find it weird?"

"No, not at all. It's pretty cool. I was just curious… "

"Well…. my dad told me last summer that me being afraid of drowning is called Aqua-phobia, and that phobia means 'fear'. So I started looking up more phobias. There are lots!" And he takes a bite of his sandwich.

Then while he's chewing says, "Like Fear of Computers is Cyberphobia, Fear of God: Theophobia, Fear of Dogs: Cynophobia… "

(Excuse me, I heard that! And I have only one word to say: Impossible!

Who could possibly fear cute furry adorable Moi?)

"Is there one for fear of other people?" Leo asks.

"I don't know. I'll check."

The bell rings to announce the next class that starts in ten minutes and they both cringe.

"P.E… " Leo sulks.

"Yeah, I… I don't feel so well. I think I better go see the nurse," Zachary says, then quickly stuffs the last corner of sandwich into his mouth while he crumbles up the brown paper lunch bag and napkin.

"No way. Not again," Leo nearly shrieks. "You can't leave me alone out there on the field!"

"Well, I was left alone last week while you were on vacation. You got to experience a cabin, woods and a lake, and I got wadded-up trash thrown at me, picked very last for basketball, and almost beat-up by Mike Monroe."

"Whatda mean 'almost'?"

"I hid in a bathroom, then rushed home the long way. He was calling me 'brain' and 'queer' and stuff… " Zachary says as he gets up. "I can't do it today. I can't… " And he walks away, leaving Leo alone on the bench, who really wishes he was an airline pilot already so he could fly away.

The nurse's office is in the Administrative building at the end of a tiled hallway with wood-paneled walls. Hanging all along the walls are framed photos of the graduating classes from Jarvis Middle School over the decades. The earlier ones from the 1940's and '50's are in black and white, and then suddenly change to vibrant colors in the 1960's. Zachary looks up at them as he passes down the long hallway, catching a few faces, and wonders if any of those kids had to put up with what he and Leo now have to.

He passes the doors marked Faculty Office, Faculty Lounge, then that of the Principal, the Vice Principal, and finally comes to the last door, that of the School Nurse. He stops for a moment and puts a tired look on his face before he knocks on the door. A voice beckons him in and he enters.

"Ah, Zachary Klossner, isn't it? Come in, dear. Sit on the bed, please," Mrs. Wells, the school nurse smiles from her desk. Her long reddish hair is pulled back behind her ears and Zachary can see that she's filling out a form or something.

"One... more... sec... " she says, then drops the pen down, swivels her chair around and rolls it closer to where Zachary sits on the edge of the bed with his head dropped down staring at the patterns in the tiled floor.

"Weren't you in last week? And a couple weeks before that?" she asks sweetly, removing reading glasses from her face that drop down and dangle from a silver chain hanging from her neck. "What is it this time—stomach? Head-ache? Muscle pain?"

"Yeah... ," Zachary mutters.

"Yeah, what?"

"The head-ache one. It's back there, I think," he says as he rubs the back of his head.

"Hmm, let me see," Mrs. Wells says as she rises up and feels Zachary's forehead, then his wrist, then the back of his head.

"Is it here?" she moves her hand down towards his neck. "Or here?"

"There, I guess. I... I think I just need to lay down."

"You mean 'lie down', dear. Lay is to put some*thing* down. Lie is to put *you* down. It's a weird quirk of English."

"My friend Leo is always telling me how weird English is... like how we say 'fear' and then how different we say 'bear' with the same spelling."

"Hmm, good point. So go ahead and LIE down, Zachary," she says, fluffing up the pillow before his head comes to rest on it. "I suppose you'll feel better at 2 o'clock."

He looks up at her, and her pale blue eyes are kind and caring, and he sort of trusts her because of that.

"I don't know how long... ," he says settling into the mattress that's covered with a single white sheet, a grey wool blanket folded perfectly at the end.

Mrs. Wells sits back at her desk and keeps her eyes on him.

"Well, I mean, it just seems that every time you come in it's Monday or Wednesday at 1 o'clock. Coincidence maybe?"

"Must be."

"What class do you have at 1 o'clock on Mondays and Wednesdays, Zachary Klossner?"

"It's Zach. I don't like my real name. It means 'sugar' in Greek."

"Oh, well, that's a pity. Some pretty talented and famous people have been named Zachary."

"Really? " he asks.

"Sure. Why, there's Zachary Quinto the young actor who plays Spock in the new 'Star Trek' films, Zachary Donahue the figure skater... um, Zachary Lemnios the scientist, and of course Zachary Taylor the twelfth president of the United States, just to name a few... "

"I didn't know... "

"So don't be ashamed of your name, or anything else about who you are, ZACHary. Now tell me—is your current class Math? History? Art? Can't imagine it's Art..."

"It's P.E., I think... "

"You think?"

"I mean, it's P.E., yeah."

"Don't you find it rather peculiar that all these illnesses you've been getting always happen before a P.E. class?" she says softly. "And I didn't see much of you last year, so I wonder why this year?"

"I dunno… "

"Hmm. Well, something to ponder. You just lie there until you're feeling better. And don't worry, you're safe here."

Zachary tenses up and raises his head off the pillow.

"Whatda mean, 'safe'? Why'd you say that?"

"I mean, it's a clinic and I'm a nurse, so it's safe just in case that headache of yours is something serious."

"Oh, that… , "Zachary replies, then relaxes again on the mattress. Really relaxes, because for the first time he does feel safe somewhere on the campus of his school.

Mrs. Wells must notice it, because she walks over and puts her hand on his head as if to check it again, but then pats his head lightly before returning to her desk to fill out a form on his visit, placing her reading glasses back on her face.

The sound of footsteps suddenly get louder as they approach from down the hallway, and Zachary immediately turns on his side away from the door to hide his face—he doesn't know who is approaching, but must always be careful not to be seen by certain students, or else!

He hears a door open further down the hall and the footsteps stop. Relieved, Zachary rolls onto his back and stares up at the patterned ceiling. Looking more intently, he can make out a figure among all the squiggles, maybe Yoda, because it seems to have big ears. Twisting his head slightly he realizes that it could also be Frodo Baggins if you use your imagination.

Looking around further he spots Gollum in another squiggle.

Then Shelob, the grotesque spider that nearly devours Frodo.

Then a creepy Orc face.

Then he sees the Nazgul, Mumakil, Crebain and Wargs....

Exhausted by all the creepy monsters, he dozes off and forgets everything.

CHAPTER 9

As soon as he leaves the Nurse's office and exits the Administrative building, three older boys spot Zachary from across the quad. Approaching him, they place their thumbs over the opening of their cola cans and shake until pressure builds up, and then as they reach him they release their thumbs from the cans, spraying syrupy cola all over him as they pass.

"Now you're really Zachary, covered in sugar, little boy," one of the tough guys snickers. The other two laugh loudly as they walk away, which other students nearby hear and look over to see what's happened. The shyer kids cower in the shadows, worried that they could be next.

Nobody, though, comes over to console Zachary.

Since he can't dare to go into a bathroom to clean up for fear of getting harassed there too, he has to attend his last class, Biology, damp with sticky cola.

Some kids in the back of the class point and snicker as he comes in and takes his seat.

There is a mid-term that day, and Zachary is luckily the kind of student who doesn't have to cram too much with his studies, and is sure he'll do well on the exam.

But when the papers are passed out on the desks, and the teacher tells them all to begin, a boy much bigger than Zachary sneaks over to the empty desk alongside him and tries to peek over at his exam as he writes. Zachary notices out of the corner of his eye and shifts in his seat to turn away and hide his answers. The other boy punches him in the shoulder when the teacher is not looking and then leans towards Zachary to whisper.

"Let me see, Klossner, or I'll cram my fist down your throat after class."

Shaking and scared, Zachary shifts back in his seat so the other boy can easily read off his paper. He can barely read the questions as he continues, and the pen shakes in his hand as he writes out the short answers, the other boy constantly peering over to copy him.

When he finishes the last question, Zachary gets up quickly and drops the exam off on the teacher's desk and rushes out the door, stumbling as he runs to the bicycle racks at the front of the school, and pedals as fast as he can, angry, hurt and scared.

And sick to his stomach of being angry, hurt and scared all the time.

When he gets home from school he doesn't tell his mom and dad about what happened in the classroom, or about the visit to the nurse, just as he hadn't told them about any of the other recent visits to her office, and manages to rush up and take a quick shower and change clothes so they won't notice the dry sticky cola all over him.

When he comes down his parents are having tea at the kitchen table and he joins them just as his father starts to outline the dumb script he had to read that day about a car that's possessed by the ghost of a serial killer and races around trying to run over people. And stray cats.

"For it seems the killer was tormented as a child by stray cats on their farm, and now, in death, seeks revenge," Mr. Klossner adds over a sip of tea.

(Ha! Did you hear that? The Dead-Killer-Car doesn't aim for just any old animals, but cats. Cats! Just goes to show you that some films do get it right:

dogs are Special Beings and no half-sane person, or even killer ghost, would aim to run over one of us.

I don't know why Mr. Klossner thinks that film is dumb. Sounds rather intelligent to me.)

Zachary reminds his dad that there was already a film about a killer car based on a Stephen King book, and another one about a killer truck that Steven Spielberg directed as his first film.

"Wow, I'm impressed you know so much about films," his dad says as he pours out more tea.

"Yeah, well, Leo and me have been watching a lot lately…." He says as he gets up to leave the table. Adding, "Oh, and there was a really lame TV movie called 'Wheels of Terror'.

"Ha! The script I read was titled 'Tires of Terror'!" Mr. Klossner says.

"Yikes!" Zachary shakes his head as he heads up the stairs.

(When Zach leaves to go upstairs to his bedroom, I instinctively follow. I can tell he's had one of those days and may need a pair of ears--or in my case, 1 ½ --to listen to his woes. But instead he gets on the computer in his parent's office and looks up things. I settle at his feet and fall asleep.)

He Googles the names of the famous people also named Zachary that Mrs. Wells told
him about and finds there are many more (including lots of TV actors), and then looks up
'Melancholy'. His dad was right: it does mean
Sad and Depressive. So he looks up Depressive.

'Causing feelings of severe despondency
and dejection,' it says.

He knows that dejection means something
like 'sad', but has never heard of Despondency, so he looks that up next.

'Low spirits from loss of hope or courage.'

Yep, that's him, he admits. He IS feeling
low. And hopeless.

Quickly he gets off that page and types in
'Limericks' to try and find something cheerful.
While it's loading up, he notices the time in the
lower corner and since his parents only allow
an hour a day on the computer, and there's just
a few minutes left, he goes instead to his usual
page that lists Phobias, and immediately spots
two new ones:

Kategelophobia—fear of ridicule
Mastigophobia—fear of getting beaten

With the pencil digging into the paper, he
writes them down to memorize later.

He puts his fingers back on the keyboard, but they suddenly tighten up. He wants to search something but hesitates, afraid that once he types it in, he brings it out in the open and makes it real.

Taking a deep breath he goes to YouTube, and slowly types 'kids picking on kids' into the search bar. A big bold word appears in the title of one of the videos that makes him freeze, and his heart starts beating wildly in his chest. He's too nervous to play the video under the heading, and instead grabs the pencil and below the two new phobias adds a single word:

BULLYING

Then he scratches it out, gets up and rushes out, calling loudly for Cassia. They both arrive at the same time to his bedroom, where he quickly slams the door shut and throws himself down on his bed just as tears start to form. He tries to stop them but they are persistent, fill his eyes, and start to run down his cheeks.

Cassia jumps up and lies next to him, licking the tears as fast as they appear.

(*And if the reason I do this is still unclear to you, please refer to a terrific and totally factual video on-line called 'And So God Made A Dog'. Respect!*)

PART TWO

ELEPHANT IS TOO BIG TO IGNORE

CHAPTER 10

Months have now passed. As have weeks, days, hours, minutes, and seconds.

For Zachary's birthday late in October he was given the choice between a party at home with as many kids as he wanted to invite, or his mother taking him into the city to see some sites, have lunch, and then a show at the Shubert theater (some musical about gangs fighting in New York in the 1950's).

Since he doesn't have many friends at school, and didn't want his parents to know about that, he chose going into the city with his mother, but asked if they could see another show—he *really* didn't want to see anything about people beating up on each other, even if they *were* singing and dancing as they did!

She tried to get him to talk over lunch near the Santa Monica pier about school and friends and his feelings, but he managed to steer the subject away, asking her about *her* school where she taught and *her* friends and *her* feelings. And although she found it odd, she was glad that he was curious and opened up a lot to her son over their meal of burgers, fries and chocolate shakes (his choice).

A few days after his birthday came Halloween, though neither Zachary nor Leo dressed up and went out trick-or-treating, afraid that they'd bump into some tough boys from school, who they heard now spend the holiday pestering younger kids and stealing their candy. It was a difficult decision to stay at home— "All that free chocolate!" Leo mourned—but they couldn't take a chance that they'd be recognized under their costumes. It was the first year Zachary did not partake in Halloween, and it made him think that maybe growing up meant you had to miss out on some good stuff, and that didn't sound very nice.

Thanksgiving then came and went as boring as always for Zachary. College football played on the TV all day (he and Tris got only quick glimpses of the Macy's parade over a French toast breakfast Mrs. Klossner made them), and their grandparents drove down from San Francisco, bringing pumpkin and mincemeat pies for the turkey dinner (the only good part of the day!)

(You can say that again! Although I love roasted dead birds, you can't beat pumpkin pie with whipped cream! Zach and Tris snuck lots of tasty bites under the table, and Mrs. Klossner let me lick the whipped cream bowl. Now that's love!)

Now it is nearing the middle of December with Christmas fast approaching, but as much as he loves this holiday best, Zachary's finding it difficult to sense any of the joy that he usually feels at this special time of year.

And the reason for that is all the uncomfortable things that have been continuing in the locker room and sports field and classrooms of his school.

('Uncomfortable'!? Uncomfortable is when the cushion you have to sleep on is all lumpy, or your collar is too tight and you're gagging, or it's a rainy weekend and you don't get to go outside for major walks and instead have to watch dumb monster movies all day with the kids.

Let's be honest here: poor Zach is more than 'uncomfortable'. He's feeling anxious and scared all the time now. I know! I hear about it when he closes his bedroom door after school with just the two of us inside. Luckily he always brings up crackers or nuts with him, so there are perks, because listening to this kid's griping all the time is getting to me. But as a dog, I must admit, my choices to alter things are limited.)

Mrs. Wells has been very nice towards Zachary the few more times that he avoided P.E. by going to her with a supposed stomach or head ache. He even pretended once to have a thorn in his toe, but when she looked for the thorn there was none and kept quiet, letting him stay until the hour was up.

What's really putting dark clouds over Zachary's Christmas enjoyment is an incident that happened last week at school.

It was during P.E. class, and as usual, he and Leo and a slightly chubby Mexican kid were picked last to be on the teams for baseball. In fact, they weren't picked at all; the two captains just stopped choosing when they were left standing alone, and Mr. Parnell forced the unwanted three on the teams.

All the boys then ran out to the baseball field, arriving long before Mr. Parnell, who stopped to answer his cell phone. Seizing the opportunity, the captain of Zachary's team, again Joe Padilla, noticed that the home base was covered with dirt.

"Guys, we need to clean the base. Let's see… who can we use to wipe it with?" and his eyes came upon Zachary, whose face suddenly went all red, his heart beating like mad.

"Johnson, you grab his arms, Katric his feet. I think a good butt-swipe might do the trick, eh guys?" Padilla grinned.

The two boys grabbed Zachary's hands and feet and lifted him into the air like a hammock, then rushed over to the home base and began swinging him, his butt lowering down, swishing the dirt off the white plastic base as it passed back and forth.

Mr. Parnell was too far to really see what was going on, but if he had, probably would have made light of it, as he always did when tougher boys bullied the younger or weaker ones.

"Part of becoming a man!" he would say in such incidents. Or "Toughens you up!"

And none of the other boys did anything to stop it either. Some were laughing and cheering, and others watched silently, backing off a bit, Leo among them, too scared to get involved or defend his best friend. He was just glad that it wasn't *him* this time!

When Mr. Parnell finally did arrive, the boys had already let go of Zachary, and he wiped the dirt off his shorts and just pretended it didn't really matter. But of course it did. He was embarrassed and hurt, but dared not show it or they would have tormented him more by calling him names.

'Sticks and stones may break my bones, but words can never hurt me,' Zachary had heard over and over since he was little. But it was a lie. Words—harsh and mean ones—DO hurt, but inside, not outside. A scrape or a cut on the arm you can put a Band-Aid on. But how to fix a wound on the *inside*?

And what had hurt him just as much was that his best friend Leo had done nothing, said nothing, while it all went on.

But then, how could he have? If he seemed in any way to be defending Zachary, they would have used *his* butt to polish the base afterwards! Zachary knew that, but it still hurt.

So things between him and Leo weren't the same since the incident a week before on the field.

Twinkling lights on the family Christmas tree are dancing in Zachary's eyes as he sits alone in the living room after school trying to conjure some joy about the holiday while his favorite CD of Christmas songs plays. Under the tree a few wrapped presents are scattered on top of the same red-and-green plaid cloth that's been laid under the trunk every year since he was a little boy, and numerous decorations adorn the room—small reindeer made of twigs on the fireplace mantle, ceramic elves on the coffee table, bits of holly perched on each picture frame, a garland of tiny red glass balls strung across the top of the large window, and a sprig of mistletoe tied with gold ribbon hanging down from the ceiling lamp.

Usually he feels such an inner happiness surrounded by all these familiar ornaments of the holiday.

But nothing was working at all to cheer him up.

Until a few days later and a visit to...

CHAPTER 11

Tante!

That's the name they use for Zachary's great aunt, and he and his family have just arrived to her house to spend an evening of pre-Christmas festivities.

When the front door to her house opens, the familiar smell of scented candles and talcum powder overwhelm him, reminding him of all the past times at her house, and instantly make him feel relaxed and loved.

There in the open doorway Tante hugs and kisses her niece, Barbara Klossner, then Mr. Klossner, Tristan, and last Zachary, who she holds onto the longest. And he doesn't mind—she is his favorite relative of all, though he feels a little guilty at the thought, and would never hurt his four grandparents or two uncles (both on his mom's side) by saying so, even if it was true. Tante is vibrant and silly and full of joy. Just what Zachary needs, especially these days.

"Oh, my, the eighth grade, Zach. And Tris, you're in High School, and what lovely pictures you're making," Tante says as she leads them all into the living room, her thick grey hair recently permed into tight curls that frame the pale wrinkly skin of her face and twinkling grey-green eyes.

"The sketch you did of Zach was wonderful! Can you make me a copy…scan it, or whatever it's called?"

"Sure, Tante," Tristan says, taking a seat on the large couch alongside her parents and little brother. "I can make you one of Cassia, too, if you want. It's only pastels… "

"Absolutely. They're all lovely. You're a talented young woman," Tante says as she rushes into the kitchen and comes out with a tray of eggnog and five glasses. She sets it down on the coffee table alongside bowls of sugared walnuts and Russian teacakes and mixed nuts, and chips with her home-made yogurt curry dip that she knows both kids love.

"Now, don't be shy. Dig in," she says as she sits in what everyone understood to be her chair: the odd overstuffed one in the corner by the fireplace covered with a nubby faded green fabric. Folded over the top is a burgundy Afghan blanket she knitted years ago when her fingers were more nimble.

"Now, Tris, tell me about high school," she asks. "Nice? Dull? Fun? Stupid? Inspiring? Any special boy?"

"Tante… ," Tristan's face turns slightly red as she picks up a curvy chip and stuffs it with a big clot of curry dip, then shoves it in her mouth.

"Well now, nothing to be shy about, honey. Maybe a special girl? I don't care, you know that. You kids can do whatever you want with your lives. As long as it fulfills you, and… ," she raises a finger in the air, "…it doesn't hurt others. Then it's fine by me."

Tristan picks up another chip, dips it, and takes a big bite.

"So, Tris, tell me! High school!" Tante tries again.

"Yeah, well, it's a bit different from Middle School, Tante. You know, the kids aren't so dippy."

"Hey!" Zachary butts in while grabbing from the bowl of mixed nuts.

"Okay, not everybody is dippy there," Tristan says with a full mouth, then swallows. "But, you know, they're more mature in high school. Kids can be so pretentious, trying to act tough and 'be somebody' in middle school.

And the classes are more interesting in high school, but way harder… My Art teacher's cool. He has his stuff up in a gallery in Portland."

"But is he inspiring you in *your* art, honey?" Tante looks directly at Tristan.

"Yeah, he does. He makes me want to be *more* of an artist."

"That's great, Tris. Really." Then to Mr. Klossner: "Mark, would you pour out the eggnog, please? Oh, Barbara, you're looking good. The teaching must be going well this term."

"It is, Tante, thanks. New students, lots of inquiries! This generation's asking a lot more questions than we did," she replies, taking a glass of eggnog that her husband hands over to her. He gives one each to Tristan and Zachary, then gets up and brings one over to Tante.

"Down the hatch," she says, and takes a big gulp. When she lowers the glass, there is a moustache of eggnog on her upper lip. Zachary giggles at this, and takes a sip from his, purposely pouring it so it covers his upper lip and he shows off his eggnog moustache too.

"You're such a darling, Zach," Tante smiles. "Did I tell you that your name means 'sugar'?"

"Many times. And Tante means 'aunt' in French. But did you know that Klossner is, like, originally German? I looked it up last week. It's spelled K-L-A-U-S then n-e-r, and means 'Hermit'. Cool, no?"

"Oh, I like that—'Hermit'," Tante replies, then takes another sip of eggnog. "I did know one side of your dad's family came from Germany. Your father's, right?"

"That's right, Tante," Mr. Klossner answers. "And my mother's side is of French nobility. Plus some Polish, I've heard. Like all Americans, we're mongrels."

(Hey, I heard that! The correct term is Unique Blend, I keep telling you!)

"Wait a sec," Tristan interrupts. "So, does that make Santa Claus, like, 'Santa Hermit'?"

"Ha, ha, aren't you funny!" Zachary sneers at his sister, then adds, "I also discovered that the name Tristan is only for boys in England," Zachary announces as he pops a Russian tea-cake into his mouth, then licks the powered sugar off his fingers. "And it means 'noise' or 'clatter'," he adds, glancing at his sister.

"Well, I looked it up, too, *Mr. Sugar*, and it can also mean 'bold'," Tristan replies. "And who cares if it's a boys or girls name. It's just a name... "

"And a wonderful one," Tante says. Then, "Hey, Zach, thanks for the Limerick you sent me. Most amusing. I hope you'll continue with writing. You're very clever!"

"Wait. What Limerick?" Mrs. Klossner says, surprised. Then turns to Zachary. "Zach, you wrote a Limerick? Why didn't I get to see it?"

"Questionable content," Tristan replies crunching on a sugared walnut.

"Meaning? Zach?" his mother continues.

"Never mind, not important," Tante intrudes. "Style and adaptability to the form was quite impressive, questionable content or not. Zach, you keep going!"

His mother nudges him with her elbow and a cashew nut spits out of his mouth onto the floor.

"Hey, Mom!"

"Sorry, but, um…. do I ever get to see this masterpiece? Honey, did he show you?" she turns to her husband.

"Me, no. I tell him all about the film scripts I have to work on, but does he show me his first poem… ?" and he pretends to cry and covers his eyes with his eggnog-free hand.

"Alright, you guys can see it," Zach concedes. "Later."

"Well, what made you decide to write it?" his father asks, recovering from his fake cry and grabbing a Russian teacake, a small cookie ball with walnuts that's been rolled in powdered sugar.

"I don't know," Zach says spotting the cashew nut on the floor and putting it back in his mouth. "Tris was talking about Art and Artists and I thought maybe I could try, too. Only I can't draw well, so I thought to write a poem, and Limericks are the only ones I know. I did… write… another one, actually… It was gonna be a surprise for while we decorated the tree."

"Oh, let's hear it, please!" his mother pleads.

"Now, now," Tante gets up and heads towards the snack bowls. "Zach wants to share it in his way. Let him." She grabs a handful of nuts and returns to her chair.

"It's okay, Tante. I can read it now, but, um, first you're gonna have to lick the eggnog off your upper lip or I might giggle too much."

She does, and Zachary's parents sit up straight as he pulls a piece of paper out of his pant pocket and unfolds it. Tris slouches on the couch.

"Okay, so I was reading about England and they say 'mum' instead of mom, and 'bum' instead of butt. And remember you told us, Mom, how your great great grandparents were from a small village in Yorkshire called Settle? So I... well, here goes."

He takes a deep breath and reads aloud.

"There was a young lad from Settle

who was constantly sitting in nettle.

Scolded by mum

for always scratching his bum,

he's now wearing trousers of metal."

Tante breaks out in a fit of laughter, and puts down her eggnog glass before it splashes all over.

"Oh, my, Zach... it... oh, my!" she snorts from laughter.

Zachary's mother pats him on the back and his father nods with a large smile. Behind their backs Tristan puts out her arm and gives Zachary a fist bump.

"A+," she says

"Do you get it?" Zachary asks.

"Oh, yes, son. We get it," his father replies still smiling. "Quite effective."

"And FUNNY, Zach!" his mom adds. "Glad to see you're having some fun."

"What do you mean?"

"Well, you…you know, you've been a bit, um… "

"Melancholy?" he asks.

"No, honey, not melancholy. But… sort of… well, sad," she says. "I've been a bit worried about you."

"Hon, he's okay. Nothing wrong with Zach," Mr. Klossner says.

"I didn't say there was anything wrong," Mrs. Klossner corrects him. "I said… "

Suddenly Tante interrupts.

"Zach, is this at all true? Is there something bothering you? I was wondering myself when you e-mailed me the Limerick with no letter. I hadn't heard from you in a while, and… "

"Hey, everything's okay!" he blurts out.

"Zach, 'Okay' is not enough," Tante says leaning forward in her chair. "Your life should be better than just okay. If it is only okay, then something *is* wrong."

He squirms in his seat.

(I could tell them! I could tell them! I know it all. But nobody ever asks the dog.

And by the way, I love eggnog, too. They better bring some home for me! And some of those Russian teacakes too, please!)

"Zach, there *is* something. What is it, son?" his dad turns to him.

"Nothing really, guys. Just… some kids at school aren't very nice… "

"What does 'not very nice' mean, Zach?" Tante asks him.

"Well…some…some of them pick on others… "

"That's part of life in Middle School, son," his dad says. "We all get picked on for one thing or another by other kids at school. They're all struggling to find their identity at that age."

"Yeah, see I told you. It's nothing." Zachary's hopeful that it is the end of the topic.

"Really, honey?" his mom says as she puts her hand on his shoulder.

"Yeah, Mom, it's okay." And he notices Tante tilt her head at him. "I mean, better than okay. It's good. Everything's good… really. Can we decorate the tree now?" he asks to change the subject before they pursue it further and he is forced to tell them everything.

"Of course we can!" Tante says getting up from her chair. "Will you kids help me get the boxes? They're in the hallway. I took them down from the attic already."

She approaches Zach as they walk into the hallway.

"Great Limerick," she says. Then quietly, so only he can hear. "And if there ever is a problem, you can talk to me anytime, Zach." And she tenderly pats his shoulder and rushes over to grab the smaller box while Zachary and Tristan carry in the heavier ones.

They place the boxes down near the tree, and Tante puts on the same old-fashioned Johnny Mathis CD of Christmas music they listen to every year when they decorate her tree, which nobody minds because it's a tradition now and brings up lots of nice memories. One by one they each carefully remove the newspaper or tissue paper wrapped around an ornament and begin to hang them all over the tree—glass, wood, ceramic, felt, and one that Tris holds up to show everyone: a pair of bells made from an egg carton, covered with gold glitter and held together with a pipe cleaner. They all smile.

Zachary made it in kindergarten and he's glad to see it again. Tristan hands it to him to put on the tree.

When the last ornaments are hanging, and the boxes empty, Tante leans down and plugs in the small white lights and the tree comes alive, sparkling and cheerful.

And for the first time in a while, so is Zachary.

CHAPTER 12

A few days before Christmas there is a knock on the Klossner's front door while they're all in the living room watching a DVD of 'A Charlie Brown Christmas'.

(I've a quick comment to make here since that particular DVD was mentioned. It's about the way you humans depict dogs in your TV shows and films. It's usually terribly insulting to us canines. I mean, Scooby Doo is dippy, Odie is annoying, Beethoven is a big slobbering Saint Bernard that causes trouble, and don't even get me started on Cujo, the rabid dog that tries to devour its owners! Sick, sick, sick.

But Snoopy! Snoopy is cool. He's the man! He's intelligent, he's insightful, he dances, he plays games, and he's friendly to Charlie Brown and all the other kids. In other words, the appropriate representation of a D-O-G.

Forget Scooby Doo and Odie.

Long Live Snoopy!

End of comment.)

Tristan gets up from the cartoon and answers the door. It's Leo, and not knowing the current situation between he and Zachary, she lets him straight in.

"Oh, hi, Leo. Zach's in the living room." Then yelling, "Zach, Leo's here."

Leo enters the living room and Mr. and Mrs. Klossner both greet him with 'Merry Christmas', and he takes a seat on the floor while Zachary ignores him, and since they are all watching the TV screen, nobody notices.

When the show is over and the adults get up and leave, Tristan asks the two boys if they want to watch another DVD, 'Frosty The Snowman' or something, and they both sort of grimace and shake their heads. Zachary heads upstairs to his room, and Leo follows a short distance behind him. He has a small wrapped present and closes Zachary's door behind him, just as Cassia sneaks in and jumps on Zachary's bed.

(*Of course I do. I'm not going to miss this awkward reunion! AND I happen to be privy to a roll of Lifesavers on the bedside table.*)

Zachary walks over to the window and pretends to look out, his back to Leo.

He's not sure what to do, or how to take this situation, because he is still hurt by Leo not defending him out on the baseball field. Or maybe he is just hurt from the whole ordeal. He can't tell anymore.

"Hey, Zach," Leo says to try and break the horrible silence between them.

"Leo… " Zach mumbles.

"I… brought you a gift. You can open it now if you want. I mean, we *are* still friends, right?"

"Yeah, I guess… I got you a gift, too. It's on the desk," Zachary says without turning around. Leo places his gift on the desk and picks up the one with his name on the tag. It's large and flat and he can't imagine what it could be.

"Can I open it now?" Leo asks.

"Sure."

Leo rips the red and white striped paper off quickly to find a large round astronomy chart with all the stars and constellations and galaxies marked.

"Wow, cool. Thanks, Zach."

"It adjusts for each period, month and stuff… ," and he reaches out and shows him how with different dials along the edges you can adjust for the time of year and region, and the stars all readjust and whirl into position.

"So that's what the night sky will look like tonight," Zach says. "I thought it'd be way cool to use up in your treehouse."

"*Our* treehouse. You helped build it." And he hands him the other present.

"Here, open mine."

Zachary pulls on the ribbon but it won't untie. He pulls harder and it won't snap either. Leo reaches for the scissors on the desk and cuts it for him. As soon as Zachary gets the paper half-way off he recognizes what's inside. It's a boxed set of 'The Lord of The Rings' trilogy in Blu-ray, and Zachary's face lights up.

"Yeah, sweet! Let's go down and watch the first one now! I saw bits of this at my cousin's, and you can actually see all the slobber on the Orcs' teeth!"

"So… we're okay. I mean, still best friends?" Leo asks.

"Yeah, I guess so. I don't have so many friends… and I've known you for eight years, and… "

Leo interrupts him.

"Dude, I'm sorry about, you know, what happened on the field last week. It was so awful, and I… I wanted to do something, really, but, I mean, if I did they would have done it to me next. I was so scared, but also, like, hurting for you. Padilla's a gorilla. Worse than a gorilla, he's, he's... "

"An Orc."

"Yeah, like an Orc, slobbery and all. He's threatened to beat me up on the way home many times...and one time in the bathroom he and some other guys tried to force me to smoke a cigarette. Called me horrible names... "

"I know. They tried that with me... "

"So, we gotta stay friends, Zach. Okay? The last two weeks with them picking on me and you ignoring me... it's been an awful Christmas."

"Yeah, for me, too."

(It's been a Great Christmas for Moi! Zach's been more desperate, and therefore more needy, and therefore I'm alone with him in his room more, and therefore LOTS MORE SNACKS! He even gave me the creamy bit from inside his Oreo the other day, and then half a granola bar! I can't say I appreciated the small candy cane bits he offered last week. I don't know what you humans get out of those! Yuck! Cheese crackers or popcorn or more Oreo guts do me just fine!)

Zachary and Leo run down the stairs with the DVD box set. Cassandra follows, nearly tripping Leo as she passes between his legs, then reaching the living room first, she aims for the couch where the two previously-sleeping cats leap off in a panic and scatter away, and she takes her place among the cushions waiting for the boys to arrive.

Before the boys even reach the bottom of the stairs Zach's screaming out,

"Mom, can Leo and I watch a film?"

CHAPTER 13

Zachary and Leo manage to get through the last days of school before Christmas vacation without any major incidents, thankful to now have two weeks of peace.

They telephone each other on Christmas morning to tell about all the gifts they'd received. Leo's favorite was a silver scooter that he'd been bugging his parents about ever since he learned that there were Scooter Competitions much like Skateboarding ones. And Zachary's was a new bicycle, since his parents finally realized that he'd had his last one since age 10, and he's sort of growing!

"It's big, Leo," he says over the phone. "Like for adults! Sort of greeny-grey color like fungus, and with mountain bike tires. I'm gonna zip way past you next time we go ride in the hills!"

"No way, man!"

"Yes, way! You haven't seen it. It's like for Green Hornet or something… "

Zachary finishes by telling all the small stuff he got in his stocking: besides candy canes…

(*Blech!*)

… and chocolates…

(Yummm!)

….there was a tangerine ("it's a family thing," he explains to Leo), a 16GB flash drive, an envelope with fifty dollars from his grandparents in Ohio, and a yo-yo.

"What's that?" Leo asks.

"Something my grandparents played with as kids. Kinda fun, I'll teach you. And the best thing was a gift certificate to Amazon! More DVDs, dude!" They cheer over this. Then he adds, "Oh, and Tris got me a pile of notebooks and a really nice pen to write more Limericks."

Suddenly Mrs. Klossner yells from the next room, so loudly that Leo can hear it over the phone.

"Zach, c'mon! We're going! Say Good-bye to Leo. Oh, and 'Merry Christmas' to him and his family. You can spend the day there tomorrow."

"Gotta go, Leo. But my mom says I can come over tomorrow. Maybe a treehouse sleepover!"

"Yeah, great," Leo replies. "I'll ask if it's okay. Have fun at your Uncle Tom's!" he adds sarcastically, knowing Zach can't stand this part of the Christmas tradition in the Klossner family.

"Fun? Ha!" he says, then hangs up the phone.

Uncle Tom and Aunt Margaret live in a small town further north along the coast. But unlike Zachary's great aunt Tante, they're no fun.

"Aunt Maggie never stops kissing me and Uncle Tom always tries to rassle," Zach complains on the drive over.

"Not to mention his pukey breath," Tristan adds.

Mrs. Klossner turns around to face the kids in the back seat.

"Guys, c'mon. Once a year it doesn't hurt to go spend some time with your relatives. My brother Tom's not the most fascinating human walking on the planet, but…"

They are driving in Mrs. Klossner's Toyota because it's becoming a bit squishy in dad's Karmann Ghia now that Tristan and Zachary are getting bigger. Zachary prefers his mom's car anyway because dad's always makes him queasy on long trips; on some of the family camping trips up in the mountains they had to stop so he could vomit on the side of the road.

The grey Toyota Corolla pulls into the driveway of a suburban house that looks almost identical to every other house on the street, and Zachary and Tristan can see Aunt Maggie through the kitchen window get all excited when she spots their arrival.

"Get ready, dear brother, " Tristan says as she pats Zachary's back while they're getting out of the car. Suddenly the front door to the house bursts open and Aunt Maggie and Uncle Tom come rushing out, she in a frilly dress and apron covered with Santa's elves, and he in a suit with a snowman pin on his lapel that lights up. Same like every year.

"Oh, oh, oh… !" Aunt Maggie squeals, her flaming red curls flapping as she runs, clapping her hands together, then holding them out before her to receive huge embraces.

Both kids try to move left and right of her advance, but she steers towards Tristan and gives her a great big bear hug, planting kisses all over her forehead and cheeks.

"Tristan in High School! I can hardly believe it! My oh my oh my!"

Meanwhile, Uncle Tom gets ahold of Zachary and squeezes so hard he can hardly breathe.

"Zach, my little man!"

They then switch off giving hugs to the other child, and Zachary can feel the slobber from Aunt Maggie's numerous cheek kisses. Plus she is rather plump, so he can barely reach his arms around her.

"Tommy," Mrs. Klossner finally approaches her brother, and she, too, is almost suffocated by his embrace. Uncle Tom's hug to Mr. Klossner is just as forceful, and eventually—bear hugs completed, faces wet with kisses—the Klossners all walk into the house, exhausted.

Zachary leans towards Tristan and whispers.

"Give me Cassandra's slobbery tongue over Aunt Maggie's wet kisses anytime."

(And, um, I'm not sure how I should take that. Is he saying that both are bad, but hers are worse? Does that mean I should/can lick him more??

In any case, I'm sort of glad to be left alone in the Klossner house now. Christmas mornings have always been chaotic and loud with every family I've been with, and though it was sort of cute when Zach buried me under all the crumpled wrapping paper and they took a dozen pictures of it and posted some on Facebook—I got 137 'likes'! My Video career is expanding!-- the older I get the more I appreciate some peace and quiet. Maybe Tristan's new obsession with Eastern stuff is rubbing off. Perhaps I'll go meditate.

UGH... !

If only they'd taken the psycho cats with them. They are presently swatting at a crumpled hunk of snowman wrapping paper back and forth across the linoleum floor of the kitchen. The kids find it funny when they do it, but I just find it annoying! How can a dog mediate with such ruckus?)

CHAPTER 14

"Gosh, golly, aren't you a looker?" Aunt Maggie says to Tristan when she hands her a marshmallow crispy square as they all gather in the living room around a huge flocked Christmas tree decorated with only purple plastic balls. "You'll be having all the boys at your feet soon enough, darling."

"And if I don't want all the boys at my feet?" she lets out of the corner of her mouth, just enough for Zachary sitting nearby to hear.

Zachary grabs another marshmallow crispy from the plate and his aunt and uncle's small dog jumps her front paws up on his knees, staring at the treat.

"Lulu, down!" Aunt Maggie yells across the room, and the little dog cowers down and sulks under the coffee table.

(Let it sulk! Dippy little thing. Do you know what kind of dog Lulu is? Well, I'll tell ya. She's not a real dog at all. She's a Shih Tzu. I know, sounds like a small car made in Japan. But it's not—it's a small creepy little thing made in China and miscalled 'a dog'.

Big bulging eyes, smashed up nose—it's sort of Gollum with fur. For most of us dogs, we don't even consider it in the same category as us. In fact, we refer to such creatures as The Icky Pooey Breeds. They include:

-Chihuahua

-Toy Poodle

-Lhasa Apso

-Affenpinscher (try to say that five times fast!)

-Pekingese

-Pomeranian

-Pug

- Shih Tzu

Now me, as I have explained before, am what you people call a mutt or mongrel, but to us dogs it is well known that we are the better dogs—more intelligent, more loyal. It's the mixed gene pool, you see. And although —if truth be told—I have a teensy-weensy bit of white poodle trash in my blood, I am mostly spaniel and retriever. What we dogs refer to as a Unique Blend.)

"It's a unique blend," Aunt Maggie says when Zachary compliments her on the marshmallow crispy just to be nice. "See, I add my own bits to the recipe: M & Ms, toasted coconut and cheerios. You won't find any like this west of the Rockies!"

"That's for sure," Tristan says under her breath. Zach smiles.

"Right. Gifts!" Mrs. Klossner announces to get things moving along. She hands a large wrapped box to her brother that's tagged for both him and his wife, and he hands it over to her to open.

"No, you, honeykins," Aunt Maggie says with a gracious smile, handing it back to him.

"I insist, Maggie-moo. You love opening gifts, and it's to us both," Uncle Tom says, also smiling, handing it back to his wife.

"Oh, darling, that's so sweet of you. But you are her brother… " passing the gift back to Uncle Tom.

"Oh, come sweetpea, you're part of the family now, too. Ain't she, Barb?"

"Of course you are, Margaret," Barbara says. "Tom's first and second wives are completely out of the picture now. C'mon, Maggie, *you* open it."

"Well, all right. If you insist," and she slowly, carefully, un-tapes the snowflake wrapping paper. Then slowly, carefully, removes it from around the box. Then slowly, carefully, refolds it and sets it aside.

"No sense in wasting," she says, same like every year.

Tristan leans over and whispers to Zach.

"Just watch. That paper will end up on your birthday gift next year."

Zachary pinches her in the arm.

Aunt Maggie sees at once what the gift is by the writing on the box --Swiss Fondue Kit— and squeals like a piglet as she rips it open to take the main pot out. It's of purple enamel.

"PURPLE! My favorite color! Oh, Barbara, bless you!" And she hands the box and pot to Tom and rushes to kiss Barbara's and then Mark's forehead.

"It's from the kids, too," Mrs. Klossner says, and Aunt Maggie plants big kisses on Zachary and Tristan and then heads for the Christmas tree.

"Thanks, Mom," Tristan leans into her mother.

Aunt Maggie returns with a large gift bag from Costco.

"And for both of you. Something practical," she says as she hands it to Barbara, who looks inside to see dozens and dozens of car fresheners in the form of various tree species and their fragrances.

"Goodness," she says as she walks over to show her husband. "Our cars will be smelling nice for the rest of our lives."

"That's the idea, Barb. That's the idea!" Maggie smiles. She then hands a box each to Tristan and Zachary. They are exactly the same wrapping paper and size.

"Now let me guess what these could possibly be," Tristan remarks privately to Zachary.

"I suddenly got Doronophobia," he whispers back. "Fear of opening gifts."

They both open together, and, of course, they both get what they get every year from Aunt Maggie and Uncle Tom: pajamas. Which wouldn't be so bad, but A) they're always polyester--"They stick to my skin," Zach complains; B) they're matching--fine when the kids were three and five years old, but now at 13 and 15 it's a bit embarrassing; and C) they are always tacky--this year they are covered with cartoon ice cream cones.

"I know how much you kids love ice cream!" Aunt Maggie says, all giggly, as they hold the pajamas up for all to see.

Mrs. Klossner nudges Zachary and he gets up to go thank his aunt and uncle for the gift. Tristan does the same, but as they pull away from Aunt Maggie she pulls them back and kisses them four or five times more on their cheeks.

"Well, then," Uncle Tom stands up. "I'm hungry. What about you Munchkins?"

And they all move into the dining room of purple striped wallpaper and a chandelier of crystals shaped like daisies. The long table is elaborately set with a green tablecloth covered in reindeer and there are sprigs of fake holly on each plate, plastic cups ("So there's no breakage!" Aunt Maggie explained years ago), and so many forks and knives and spoons at each place setting that the kids always have to watch their aunt and uncle to know which utensil to use for which serving.

"At least she makes a killer turkey and dressing," Tristan says to Zachary as they take their places at the table, which are labeled with angel place cards.

Zachary notices that Tristan has taken the place labeled for him and he's now forced to sit at her place, next to Aunt Maggie.

"Hey!" he whispers to her. She grabs the two place cards with their names and switches them without anybody noticing.

After the meal comes three different pies, and after that comes Christmas carols. No, not on the radio or a CD, but provided by the kids. It's Zachary's least favorite part of an already

irksome tradition, because he is always expected to sing one song solo, though at least they
let him pick the song.

He chooses 'Away in the Manger' because
it's the shortest one he can think of, and though
he has to sing in a slightly lower key than usual
as his voice is beginning to change a bit, and he
also misses the high note, he is barraged with
kisses from his aunt.

Luckily, soon after the carols, they pack up
and leave—more kisses good-bye—and head
back home, taking a windy route through town
to see all the pretty lights people have strung
up on their houses. Zachary slumps down low
in the backseat when they are in an area near
where Padilla lives, for fear of being seen.

Once back home they have more eggnog
and settle down in the living room for their
Christmas Night ritual: a showing of 'It's a
Wonderful Life', an old Hollywood movie in
black and white about a man who gets frustrated with his life and wants to die, until a
guardian angel appears and shows him how
horrible it would have been for others had he
never been born at all.

It's a little old-fashioned--"Sorta lame," Leo
once commented-- but Zachary and Tristan

enjoy it every year, and now their new dog Cassia does too.

(Hey! Don't put words in my mouth. I don't actually enjoy this film—no dogs in it!—but rather the lingering cuddles I get whenever they all sit still for two hours to watch a DVD.

And let me just say it here and now:

BAH HUMBUG on your Christmas tradition!

It is full of animals—plastic reindeer on front lawns, sheep and cows at the manger, camels with the wise men-- but some how, some way, the dog species has been totally white-washed out of the story. I'm telling you, if a precious saintly baby was born, there was a dog (two or three possibly!) nearby, for sure. You ought to have a statue of a dog (might I suggest a Unique Blend) in the nativity scenes licking baby Jesus' face, because that's how it would have happened!

I've heard that you actually do have a saying, 'The dog in a manger', but as usual when you refer to my species it is not very nice, so we won't go into it.)

CHAPTER 15

The next afternoon, December 26th, Mark Klossner is watching a documentary on TV with Cassia on his lap and the two cats flopped over the headrest, Barbara Klossner is writing out thank you e-mails on the computer for all the gifts received, Tristan is upstairs trying to get into meditation, but is constantly distracted by ideas for new paintings and having to get up to make quick doodles, and Zachary is on his new grey-green bicycle riding over to Leo's. A stark low winter sun is out, the air is fresh, and he likes navigating the long stretches of the streets and curves with his new bike, bouncing up and over curbs along the way, suddenly feeling like he is 9 or 10 years old again without any problems at all.

He has on a small backpack for a sleepover with his toothbrush inside, a flashlight, pajamas (no, not the new ice cream cones ones from Aunt Maggie), and all of the milk chocolate from his stocking to give to Leo, because he only likes dark chocolate these days but his parents keep forgetting.

When he arrives, Leo rushes out to see the new bicycle.

"Wow! Cool! I wonder if it comes in black? I want a black one with silver seat and hand grips, like a Batmobile... or I guess it'd be called a Batcycle."

Zachary lets him ride it in a small circle on the driveway, then insists on putting it in the garage for safe-keeping. So they enter the house through a door in the back of the garage, passing through the laundry room, the kitchen (where they grab Christmas butter cookies from the C3PO cookie jar), and then up the stairs to a nook in the landing where the computer is kept. Leo grabs a second chair from his room and they sit in front of the computer, Zachary showing him the website where he gets all the Phobia names from, and Leo locating a video on YouTube he discovered recently where assorted cats are trying to leap onto things, miscalculate, and end up crashing into walls and windows. One lands in an aquarium. another is left hanging from a ceiling lamp. They both laugh out loud a lot and munch on the crumbly butter cookies, Leo quickly blowing crumbs off the keyboard so his father won't yell at him later.

(I'd be laughing out loud, too--ridiculous feline creatures!--except that dogs can't laugh. Yet! And it's truly beyond me why cat videos are the most popular on the Internet! Really, what's wrong with you people?)

Leo then finds an on-line video game where you're supposed to pilot military helicopters on intricate missions, but they instead have more fun purposely crashing them.

Mrs. Werner soon yells up.

"Time's up on the computer, you guys. C'mon, you know the rule."

They quickly load up and crash one more helicopter each, then shut off the computer and settle in his room on the top bunk with a new set of 'Star Wars' cards that were a gift in Leo's stocking.

Leo had hesitated a moment before climbing up, and Zachary figured it's because it was where his brother Gordon slept, and Leo probably misses him most at the holidays.

"The new film was way better than the last three," Zachary remarks as he flips through the cards looking for one of Kylo Ren and trying to make Leo think of something besides his brother.

"Oh, god, yeah. Jar Jar Binks was like, totally obnoxious," Leo agrees.

"So was that little kid who played Anakin. What a dweeb. Only the pod race was good in that one."

"I still like the first three best. They were funnier, even if some of the special effects were, like, lame."

After a dinner of leftover turkey, stuffing, mashed potatoes, green beans, and again, pumpkin pie with whipped cream, this time from a can ("My mom's is way better. She makes her own whipped cream," Zach remarks when Mrs. Werner can't hear), the two boys brush their teeth and then turn on their flashlights and make their way out and across the back lawn to the large oak tree where the treehouse they built and keep adapting has been for years. Luckily the weather is mild in California, even in winter, so they can sleep outdoors with no problem.

They use the four small boards nailed to the trunk for steps to get to the lowest branch, where they can then easily climb branch-to-branch up to the door of the treehouse and then close it behind them, latching it with a piece of twine that wraps around a nail.

When Leo and his dad renovated it last year, they put a large piece of plexiglass as part of a roof, so sunlight comes in during the day, and at night you can see a swatch of the sky and stars.

"So did you bring the star chart I got you?" Zachary asks as they turn on the two solar-powered lanterns and start to unpack their backpacks. Mr. Werner and Leo had come up earlier that day and laid out mats and sleeping bags and pillows, as well as bringing two bottles of water and the lanterns.

"Of course I did," Leo answers as he goes into his bag and starts removing what's inside: sunflower seeds, a bag of barbeque chips, chocolate bars and a Coke he took from the frig.

"Ta da!" he says pulling the chart out.

Neither change into the pajamas that both parents insisted they bring, but kick off their shoes and wriggle into the two sleeping bags fully clothed.

"Lift up the chart," Zachary says, grabbing the lantern and holding it up as Leo brings the chart near.

"So, we set it for late December, Northern Hemisphere, and, look, we should be able to see the Orion constellation somewhere." They put down the chart and look up, but can't see anything of the night sky through the glass.

"Oh, how stupid!" Zachary says as he turns off the lantern. In a few moments their eyes adjust to the darkness and they can start to make out stars way up in the sky.

"Hmm, can't see that Orion pattern," Zachary says. "It's usually very clear. My dad points it out all the time whenever we're out at night. Let's shift." And they squirm in their sleeping bags until they slide across the floor into new positions, looking up now from different angles at the sky.

"Oh, oh, there it is. I see it!" Zachary nearly shouts.

"Where?"

Zachary leans his head in towards Leo's until they are touching and points up through the large skylight.

"Look. See those three stars in a row?"

"No. Where? Which three… oh, wait… yeah, I see them now!" Leo says all excited.

"That's the belt of Orion the Warrior," Zachary explains. "There's some, like misty stars coming down from that, that's his sword.

And in there is the Orion Nebula of all these gases where, like, new stars are born."

Leo stares in awe for a moment, then lowers his head more comfortably into his pillow.

"I wish I was a warrior," he says.

"More than a Superhero? I mean, would you choose being, like, a knight or a warrior or something over Superman or Ironman?"

Zachary tilts his head to look over at Leo, their eyes only inches apart.

"Well, maybe not instead of Superman," Leo finally answers. "But if I had powers I could stop the bad guys."

"Yeah, that'd be great, huh?" Zachary says folding his arms back behind his head and still looking up at the stars. "What would you do to the bad guys if you could?"

"Smash 'em like bugs. You?"

"I'd stop them first from hurting people," Zachary says. He thinks a minute. "Then, I don't' know… make 'em see how it feels to be hurt by other people so they'd know."

"Know *what*?" Leo asks.

"Know how bad it feels."

"Yeah, that's true… Sometimes I think if my brother Gordon was here, he'd be 17 now and could protect me."

"Can we talk about something else? We're on vacation from all that and I don't wanna think about it right now," Zachary says, moving his head away from his pillow.

"Okay, what about "The Hobbit Part One'? Did you see it on TV last night?" Leo asks.

"No. Dad wanted to watch something on Terrorism, so I went up and tried to write another Limerick. Besides, 'The Hobbit' isn't as good as 'Lord of the Rings'."

"Yeah, true. So… let's hear your Limerick."

"I could only do the first two lines. I'll finish it later. It's about Cassandra."

"A dog Limerick? Oh, c'mon, Zach, let me hear it."

"I told you, I only did the first two lines."

"So, let me hear the first two lines then. Please…"

"Ugh! Okay, okay… wait… I have to remember it… Okay, here goes:

There was a cute mongrel named Cassy
Who, when taunted, could get rather sassy…"

"Ha! Nice," Leo laughs, punching Zachary lightly in the side. And they start tickling each other through the sleeping bags, squirming and giggling loudly under the starry sky, knocking over the lantern and smashing the bag of chips.

(Hey, I heard that Limerick fragment. Really! We dogs often have a psychic connection to the people we are most connected to. I had it with my last owner's daughter, and now it's getting stronger with Zach. Which makes sense since I recently found out that the Greek princess Cassandra that I am named after was also a Prophet! She could see into the future and stuff, so maybe that explains my unusually strong psychic gift!

Though I must say: I'm not sure I like being called Sassy!)

CHAPTER 16

Neither Zachary nor Leo get much sleep overnight in the treehouse. They're too scared of every little scratchy sound or creaky noise or movement of wind in the tree branches and end up telling each other jokes and tossing and turning and tossing again all night. They considered climbing down and running through the dark into the house and back to Leo's bunk bed, but they discussed it and figured that both now being thirteen years old they had to stop being so afraid and confront their fears. So although they did not sleep well, at least they stayed up in the treehouse all night for the first time without chickening out.

(There you go, doing it again! Dragging us animals into your dumb sayings. Poor chickens!

Which reminds me, I'm in the midst of compiling a list of sayings where you use the D-O-G name in vain. I'll get back to you later with it, so watch this space.)

Climbing down early in the morning, Zachary grabs onto one of the lower branches and swings wildly before making a large leap on the dewy grass.

"No wonder Tris calls you 'Monkey' some-times," Leo says, carefully scooting himself down onto the four planks of wood, then step-ping very slowly onto the ground.

Once back in the house, Mrs. Werner makes them a special breakfast of eggs, sausage and toast as a reward for their bravery in staying all night in the treehouse. Even Mr. Werner was surprised that they made it through the night and did not come rushing in to sleep indoors.

"Good for you boys,' he pats them on their shoulders while they're eating when he arrives in the kitchen. "See! It's always good when you face up to your fears. Next time you'll sleep even better up there, I bet."

Zachary arrives home in the afternoon af-ter spending the rest of the morning remov-ing all their stuff from the treehouse and then throwing a Frisbee back and forth with Leo in the backyard until Mr. and Mrs. Werner take them out for a pizza lunch.

He goes immediately up to his room and falls asleep trying to work out his new Limerick about Cassia.

When he wakes up a couple hours later, Cassia flopped over his legs and snoring...

(I Am Not!)

... he grabs one of the new notebooks that Tristan gave him and looks at what he had written for the new Limerick.. Frustrated that the middle bit and ending are not coming together, he crosses all the lines out, and then again, and then harder and harder until the pen rips through the paper. Shocked when he sees what he had done, he rips the page out, crumbles it up and throws it on the floor.

(Meanwhile, I am pretending to be asleep because his behavior is freaking me out. I should wriggle up towards his head and lick his face at such a time, but he's reminding me too much of my first owners and their aggression, so I just lie here quietly and try to ignore him, one eye slightly open at all times in case I miss something.)

On the new page Zachary begins all over and decides to make the Limerick about dogs and reincarnation, a topic his sister discusses a lot these days since she is reading all these books on Hinduism and Buddhism.

'If Cassia is good in this life maybe she'll get to come back as a human,' he considers, and writes down the word 'human' and then goes through the alphabet in his head to find words that rhyme.

Assuming. Blooming. Dooming. Fuming. Grooming. Looming… that's all he can think of, and is surprised there's nothing starting with R or S or T.

Back and forth he works on the poem's five lines, three of which must follow one rhyming pattern—that's where the 'human' words will be used, he decides—and then two short middle lines with a different rhyme, which he already decided would be 'karma' and 'dharma', the words Tristan told him mean 'fate' and 'the path' in Eastern philosophy.

Many attempts. Many scribblings. Many scratched-out lines. He sits up with his pillow behind his head and tries again.

'Darn! Art's not easy!' he moans to himself.

(So why do you think us dogs don't even attempt making Art? Our 'art' is our Beingness. Go look on YouTube if you don't believe me. Thousands of videos of dogs just Being Dogs. Millions of hits and even more Likes. Who needs pen and paper or paint brush and canvas when you're as naturally gifted as our species?)

Suddenly the middle bit comes to Zachary:

'that by following the dharma
she might increase good karma… '

But the first two lines are still not working in the rhyme necessary for the Limerick. He's about to toss the notebook aside and give up, when he remembers what his math teacher once said about 'making an effort to make things happen'. So he opens back up to the pages he's been writing on and ponders the words again.

Then he puts down the pen and closes his eyes, taking a few really deep breaths as Tristan had taught him to do in times of stress.

He opens his eyes and looks back down at the notebook. At once he sees what's not working and rewrites the opening line, adapts all the others to match it, and lays the notebook down on his lap slowly and reads the new Limerick.

A quite clever dog was assuming
as her mystical dog-thoughts were blooming,
that by following the dharma
she might increase good karma
and get to come back as a human.

He grabs the pad and leaps off his bed, runs to the door, opens it, and rushes across the hall to share it with Tristan.

(Excuse me! But since the inspiration was Moi, I'm 'assuming as my dog-thoughts are blooming' that my input is warranted and valid.

Well, here it is:

Phooey!

Okay, Zach gets an A+ for execution, but a D- for any sense of Reality!

I hate to break the news to you humans, but you've got it all wrong regarding Reincarnation. You think that the final goal is to come back as a human, but you be-lieve that because…you're human! What egos!

Now consider this: a dog gets free food, lots of free cuddles, goes on holiday with their owners (and doesn't have to pay the bill), can pee and poo anywhere they want outdoors, AND can lie around all day and sleep. A perfect life. A privileged life. A REWARDED life. The ideal final reincarnation!

So according to us, if you are a good human in this life and you're lucky (and I mean really REALLY lucky) you get to come back as a dog!

Unless, of course, you happen to be born in China, where they eat dogs.)

CHAPTER 17

A few days after Christmas and before New Years Day, Zachary and Tristan cycle over to the nearby outdoor mall with three purposes: to return a gift, to secretly get a donut each since their parents won't buy them anymore because they're too unhealthy, and to see what's playing at the cinema in case they want to get away from any boring New Year's festivities.

"Donuts first," Zachary says as they lock their bikes in one of the many bike racks.

"I'm getting chocolate glazed. The big one. You?" he asks.

"Can't decide between a cinnamon roll or a coconut donut," Tristan says as they start walking quickly past all the storefronts to get to their first destination.

She decides on coconut at the donut shop, and they eat them as they walk over to the cinema to check times on the new films playing, and then towards the huge electronic store that sells DVDs. There they hope to return a boxed set of the 'Twilight' series that their grandparents up north mailed Tristan for Christmas.

"Seriously?" she'd remarked when she unwrapped it on Christmas morning. "A girl would fall in love with a vampire and actually *become one* for him?? I don't think so. Lame idea."

"Now, Tris. Your grandparents thought you might like it," Mrs. Klossner tried to calm her.

"Yeah, and what does that say about what they think of me? That I condone cross-creature relationships? "

"Well, hon, you can go and exchange it next week if you want."

Which is exactly what she intends to do as she and Zachary arrive to the huge computer store at the far end of the mall, wiping any donut residue off their fingers onto their pants as they push open the glass doors.

They separate at the DVD section, each wandering down different rows, looking up and down the many shelves for ideas.

"Hey, what about 'Snow White and the Huntsman'? Zachary yells to Tristan from the next row over.

"Creepy 'Twilight' chick does post-modern fairy tale? I don't think so," Tris yells back. Then, "Zach, did you see 'Maze Runner'?"

"First or second," a voice comes from further down the next row.

"First."

"Yeah. Kinda naff. Some guys are caught in the center of this maze thing in some distant future, and there are monsters. Oh, and a girl suddenly shows up. Oh, and there's a twist ending."

"More 'Hunger Games' rip-off stuff, huh?"

" 'fraid so."

They both continue looking up and down the many shelves on their rows, picking up assorted DVDs out of curiosity and to get ideas for Tristan to exchange with.

"Hey, what about the original 'Charlie and the Chocolate Factory'?" Zachary's voice suddenly suggests. "Leo said it was way better than the remake. Or… oh, oh, how about the new 'Planet of the Apes'? They filmed it in the woods up near San Francisco. Supposed to be okay."

"More like a film for you and Leo," Tristan replies. "Maybe something about Art. I heard there's a good French film on Van Gogh."

"French?!" Zachary screeches. "How are you gonna understand it?"

"Subtitles, dork. Hello!"

"Oh, yeah. Forgot. Hey, remember when you took me to see this?" Zachary says, holding a DVD up high so it appears above the shelves to where Tristan is standing. It's 'Speed Racer'.

"Oh, god. Awful. Who would've guessed from 'The Matrix' dudes?"

"By the way, they're not dudes anymore. One of them changed into a woman."

"Yeah, I heard. That's cool," Tris says. "But 'Speed Racer' was still awful!"

"I rather liked it," a large bearded man looking at DVDs near Tristan comments.

"Sorry… ," Tristan says, and moves further along. Then under her breath, "But it *was* awful."

"Ooh, ooh, Tris, what about this? AND it's a boxed set."

Tristan looks up and over the low shelves at what her brother is holding, but can't make it out except for the image of a knife on the cover.

"Can't see," she says.

"Hitchcock collection," Zachary says. "Isn't he the dude who did 'The Birds'? That was cool. Remember when the guy's eyes are all pecked out? It says on the back that it includes, um, 'Psycho', 'Vertigo' and 'Marni'."

"Oh, god, no thanks. 'Psycho' is the one where that lady stops at a motel and some weirdo guy who has mother issues stabs her in the shower. Thanks, but no thanks." And she kneels down to peer at the lower shelves in her row, losing sight of Zachary completely.

"'Home Alone 1,2 and 3'"? Zachary's voice yells from a couple rows over.

"I'm fifteen, Zach, not seven!"

"'American Pie 1, 2, and 3'?"

"And I'm an intelligent fifteen. That's for pathetic teenaged boys."

"Hey!" Zachary bellows back.

"Present company excluded."

"James Bond collection"? his voice suddenly asks.

"Which ones?"

"The Roger Moore ones."

"Oh God, please! Dreadful." Then she spots one that interests her called 'The Girl With the Pearl Earing' about an artist, and asks Zachary if he's heard of it. But there's no reply.

"What, is it that bad?" she says. "Zach? Hey, Zach, yes or no?"

Still no reply. So she rises and moves down along her row and into the next row. It is empty, but she can hear some aggressive voices from one row over, and moves along, suddenly recognizing Zachary's pleading voice. She rushes quickly to the next row, where she finds him kneeling on the ground with two taller, tougher boys hovering over him, one pulling DVDs out from the shelves. It is Joe Padilla, from Zachary's school.

"What about 'Barbie Goes on Vacation'? Or 'Little Pony'?" he says tossing the DVDs on Zachary's head. "Oh, and of course, 'Pretty in Pink'."

"Hey!" Tristan says forcefully. "What do you think you are doing to my brother?"

"Oh, Zach's sister comes to help him out," Padilla says. "Ain't that sooo sweet."

"Leave him alone, you sorry excuse for humans!" she adds, bending down to help Zachary up.

"Okay, if big sis says so," Padilla adds sarcastically, dropping the last DVD on Zachary's head then wandering away, snickering with his friend.

"A-holes!" Tristan yells back at them, then grabs Zachary by the shoulders and helps him to his feet.

"Do you know those creepers, Zach?"

"One. From school," he says, trying to act brave like it didn't really matter. But his heart is racing and he's embarrassed, and worse, that his sister witnessed what he's been suffering for months. Worse still, Padilla saw her defend him, and that will be all around school when vacation's over.

"C'mon, let's go," Zachary says. "Out the back way."

"But I didn't decide which DVD to get."

"Get the James Bond set that includes 'Die Another Day', 'cuz that's how I'm feeling."

CHAPTER 18

When Zachary and Tristan arrive home from the mall, their mother pops her head out from the kitchen.

"So? How'd it go? Find some better DVDs?"

"No, not really… I'll go back again another time," Tristan replies pulling Zachary towards the stairs.

"You kids had hours to look. It might not be so easy to exchange them another day, Tris. Without a receipt, you know, well, you get a bit of leniency just after Christmas… "

"We got distracted," Tristan says.

"Good distraction, I hope." Mrs. Klossner says as she pops her head back into the kitchen out of view.

"Not so good… " Tristan says, and Zachary hits her lightly with his palm.

"You promised not to tell," he moans.

"Huh? What was that? Didn't hear… ," comes their mother's voice from the kitchen.

"Nothing, Mom," Tristan replies as she starts up the stairs, grabbing Zachary by the shirt collar and pulling him along. A moment later Cassia follows, squeezing through the doorway to Tristan's room just as the door closes.

"Right. Sit down, Zach. Tell me. How long's this been going on?"

He sits on the end of her bed, and she settles into the chair at her desk. Cassia then settles on the floor, pretending to be asleep, but all one-and-a-half ears are listening.

"Awhile… a bit last year in seventh grade, but more and more this year."

"Zach, it's called Bullying, and it's wrong. You have to report it!"

"Ha! Right! Like anybody cares. The P.E. teacher encourages the bullies, and the other kids, they… I mean… " And tears start to form in his eyes.

"Then you need to report that, too. Honest, Zach, this can't go on."

"You're telling me! But one thing you don't get, Tris. If I tell, the bullies get called in, warned maybe, and then they are WORSE!"

"Yeah, true. I saw a kid in ninth grade… "

"You mean this goes on in ninth grade, too? Ah, god… " And Zachary drops his head down onto his knees.

"… not as much, Zach, no. Most kids have matured by then, you know, out of infancy. But this one kid, Nathan, he was a bit nerdy. Okay, he was *very* nerdy, and the other guys used to make such fun of him all the time—in the cafeteria, in the quad, the corridors, outside class. God only knows what went on in the locker rooms."

"It's the worst in P.E., trust me."

"Yeah, guys seem to think their worth is based on how well they hit a ball or dunk a basket. Lame."

"Not all guys think that," Zachary interjects.

"No. And that's the point, Zach. If you are different, in any way, from the norm, the norm tries to make you adapt. Forces you!"

"But I don't want to adapt and be like that. I mean, what does kicking a ball have to do with the rest of your life?"

"Nothing. Absolutely nothing. But most guys are led to believe that manhood equals aggression. Maybe leftover from caveman times or something…"

"Yeah, but HELLO, we've moved on way past living in caves… or so I thought."

"Hey, it's just as tough for us females. It's assumed we're all sweet and gentle and passive.

That's why many guys and girls don't like me, Zach."

"Yeah, but you don't get constantly picked on for it."

"Well, define 'picked on'. But it's true: guys are much worse in that way than girls. It's a macho thing. A stupid guy thing."

"Stupid or not, it hurts. It says on-line that 45% of kids are bullied every day. Everyday! 70% actually considered changing their appearance to fit in better, and 24% felt suicidal after being picked on," he tells her through his tears. Then adds, "The experts say that the findings are 'deeply worrying'. Yeah, right. Nobody seems to really care at all what we're going through out there! It's like a mini warzone."

Tristan gets up and reaches over to hug her little brother. Cassia sees this and wags her tail. Zachary can hear it thumping on the floor.

"Zach, listen to me. You're okay just the way you are. And don't you let anybody, ANYBODY, make you think otherwise. They can try to beat your sweetness out of you, but they're probably just jealous that you're such a nice guy and those bullies are not."

Zach raises his head, tears still falling down his face.

"Thanks, Tris, but it's me who has to go back into the lion's den next week when school starts." And he gets up to leave.

"Tell somebody at school, Zach! You must!"

"WHO? Who can I trust?"

"Find somebody! There must be someone… "

He reaches the door and turns around.

"Remember: not a word to Mom and Dad. I don't want them to worry."

"Promise," she says.

"I guess I can thank god I'm not on Facebook or Twitter or that other one."

'What do you mean?"

"I hear bullying is ten times worse on-line. Imagine Ten-Times-Worse than Worst!"

And he slowly turns and leaves.

(Did I hear him say 'back into the Lion's den'? Again with the animal metaphors. Leave us out of your human dramas!

And Ten-Times-Worse than Worst must be, um… Worstest!)

CHAPTER 18½

After Zachary left the room, my tail stopped wagging. My heart started beating wildly instead. And I realized why.

I have a confession. I simply can't avoid it anymore. Zach's trust in finally opening up about what he's going through, his bravery, has inspired me. So here goes:

THE REAL PLIGHT OF BOBOLINA

For a long time I have been saying that my past-past-past owners, the Heffernans, the ones who called me Bobolina, were a bit mean to me once in a while, and that one day up on Big Elk mountain with them I accidently got abandonded and lost half my ear from frost bite.

Well, that's not true.

The truth is, they started to be mean ALL THE TIME.

They hit me endlessly. Early on it was with a rolled-up newspaper, and then their bare hands. I can understand why they did on the day I gnawed on Mr. Heffernan's $100 leather shoes, or Mrs. Heffernan's favorite cushion or peed yet again on the living room *carpet, although in my defense, I was still technically a puppy at the time, and you humans put diapers on small kids for a reason: uncontrollable bladders. Well, it's the same for us dogs when we're puppies. When the pee's gotta dribble out, it dribbles out! We haven't learned yet exactly which muscle to switch on to control it like a faucet. That comes later, about the same time we learn that swallowing bits of chewed-up cushion can cause constipation, so we stop doing it (swallowing the bits, that is. We don't stop chewing up things that are really fun to chew up, ever!)*

They also used to hit my butt when I squealed at night. But, c'mon, you can't lock a puppy alone in a laundry or bathroom. We're at our most vulnerable and helpless, and that means Needy! Remember, we used to roam around in large packs back when we were wolves (thankfully, there were no poodle or chowchow versions of us back then!) so we want company. A cat you can leave on its own for long periods, they don't care (silly creatures!), but we dogs, puppies especially, we want our pack, and You Guys Are Our Pack!

Keeping Dogs As Pets 101:

1—You can't leave a dog alone for many hours. We freak out. (Scientists have done tests that show we actually go into panic mode.)

2—We don't learn by being hit over and over. Try kibble rewards instead!

So, yeah, they hit me for relying on my basic wolf instincts of Needing Company.

They also used to yell at me if I rushed in the kitchen when Mrs. Heffernan was making nice smells with her cooking. Imagine: your mom's baking chocolate chip cookies and bans you from a twenty- foot radius. No wooden spoon or bowl to lick. No hunk of raw cookie dough. CRIMINAL!

Well, I'm sorry, when I smell beef bits frying for a stew or chicken roasting, my nose tells my brain to tell my feet to Get In There Quick! So I used to rush in (Okay, so sometimes I used to jump up on Mrs. Heffernan's legs to make my point clear that the beef bits or chicken smelled mighty appealing and might I get a wee sample?), and she would yell at me, LOUDLY! And if I insisted, she'd slap my butt, HARD, and call me 'Bad Doggie!' which, as I grew, became 'Bad Dog!', which became, when she was really pissed off, 'Bad Bobolina!'

Eventually I withdrew and got a negative self-image. Even their kids had tired of me, and stopped playing with me. (It wasn't until I was saved by my second family, the Godots, and got lots of love there, that I grew into the wonderful adorable wise creature you find me today. But that's a side-note. Anyways, back to my childhood…sorry, my puppyhood.)

It was cold, dark and blustery when the Terrible Day occurred, (actually, I don't remember the weather that day, but it helps create mood), and Mr. Heffernan let me out of the bathroom where he'd kept me for two days simply for chewing (which evolved into ripping-to-shreds) his favorite underpants. How was I to know that he preferred the ones that said 'I Love Ya, Baby' on them?

All the kids were away at their grandma's for the week, and he immediately whisked me into the car, using a fake smile to trick me when, really, he still held a grudge over The Underpants Incident. I leapt in the back loyally, gladly, thinking maybe he forgave me and was taking me to the park for a run, or better, that he felt guilty about over-reacting and was taking us both to Starbucks, he for a grande double decaf Frappuccino, and me for the free dog treats they give out at the counter.

But we drove for quite a while, past at least four Starbucks, I counted out the back window. Far from town, then far from civilization, up and up into the hills we went. 'Oh, boy!' I thought. 'Forget the park or Starbucks. He's taking me for a mountain hike, so badly does he want to make up for abusing me!'

Then suddenly he pulled over in what seemed like the middle of nowhere—no cross roads, no pathways, no signs—opened up the back of the car and proceeded to take off my collar. That's when alarm bells went off in my head.

'Uh, oh, Bobolina. This ain't lookin' so good,' a voice in my head whimpered. 'On that collar is the tag that has your name and telephone number on it. Without it, you're just 'dog' or 'doggy' or 'Hey, you'.

"Come out! Now!" Mr. Heffernan then yelled, pointing to the ground outside the car.

I refused, naturally. Something was up, and it didn't smell good. (I use the term 'smell' here metaphorically. Of course you can't smell fear or danger the same way you do beef bits or roasting chicken.)

"Bobolina, out now!!" he repeated with not the pleasantest of voices. It was, in fact, the last time he, or anybody for that matter, called me Bobolina.

I cowered, crawling as far back as I could until the back seat stopped me. I may have even piddled in fear, if truth be told.

"Out! NOW!" he yelled ever louder, which scared me even more. Trouble, I knew, was brewing. (Again, notice my clever use of metaphor—trouble doesn't actually brew like coffee does.)

Then suddenly, aggressively, Mr. Heffernan reached in and grabbed me by the scruff of my neck (you know, that extra flabby bit that we dogs have), and yanked me.

I resisted. My claws scraped across the black polyester carpet. But he pulled hard, and my head bashed *against that thick strip of metal that hangs down to open and close the trunk door, tearing into my left ear and nearly ripping it off.*

I yelped.

He yelled.

Finally he managed to pull me to the edge, and in one grab-pull-lift he had me out and threw me (THREW! MOI!) onto to the ground. Stunned by the sudden turn of events (so much for the 'I'm-sorry-Starbucks-treats'!), and feeling pain in my ear, I struggled to get up just as Mr. Heffernan got back in the driver's seat, started the car engine and drove off.

'Ouch,' I said to myself, 'that hurts'. Meaning the torn ear AND the abandonment. Suddenly it seemed I was homeless, nameless, and half-earless.

But we dogs have a bravery and determination that defies logic. And more importantly, we have what we re-fer to as PPP, Perfect Perception of Place. It's what you humans call our incredible radar sense that allows us to retrace old steps even if we haven't personally taken them. There are true stories (and a rather dorky Disney film) of dogs who have been accidently left behind by their owners when they move across country, and three months later the pet dog will show up at the doorstep of the new house, miles and miles away!

Now that's PPP in action.

My PPP though, I must confess, is not the best. (I think the poodle part in my genes diffused it a bit.) For example, when I was accidently left at a park by the father of my second family (which you can read all about in the first book I wrote with a little help from two sympathetic humans), I admit that I had just a wee bit of trouble finding my way home.

But what I lack in PPP I make up for in Adorableness!

Eventually I had enough PPP to find my way down from Big Elk mountain after Mr. Heffernan abandoned me, and was saved by some nice folks at an animal shelter who kindly removed the dangling bit of ear-tip which couldn't be saved, and fed me until the Godot family came in and took me and gave me a home.

And they were much kinder than the Heffernan's, especially the daughter, Danielle, who gave me the most attention, my name, and scraps of food under the table!

Keeping Dogs As Pets 101:

3—Don't take a puppy from a shelter or a box at the supermarket if you don't intend to keep it and be nice to it.

4—Keep your favorite underpants out of your dog's reach at all times.

5—Scraps of food under the table are a sure way to a dog's heart.

So, there, I admit it now. I wasn't accidently lost on the mountain, I was intentionally abandoned. And I didn't lose my ear from frost-bite as I earlier documented. It was taken off when I was being…..

BULLIED!

There, I said it. The B Word. I, too, was a victim of bullying, and suffered the humiliation and confusion and self-doubt that it causes. And I've been thinking a lot about it lately while watching Zachary go through his difficulties, and I think that it had an imprint on my life and on becoming ME. There is a notion coming from you humans that Good Can Come Out Of Suffering, that we grow when we overcome something uncomfortable.

Well, with lots of love and care from kinder owners, I grew into wonderful, clever ME!

End of my short story.

PS—I found out that the name 'Heffernan' is Irish and means 'demon'. I'll vouch for that!

PPS—You can read about that life-defining incident and many others in my upcoming memoir titled 'From Bobolina To Cassandra—A Dog's Life in Transition."

CHAPTER 19

It is now the last weekend of Christmas vacation. New Year's has come and gone with the usual occurrence: everybody in the Klossner family vowed to stay up and watch the fake fireball drop from Times Square in New York, but halfway through watching 'Gladiator' —"We need a long epic film to fill the time," Zachary had suggested—both Zachary and his mother fell asleep, only to be awakened when firecrackers start going off in the neighborhood and startled them.

Their grandparents from up north phoned shortly after midnight, and when Zachary was called to the phone, he was glad that his grandma didn't ask him about school because he was tried of lying and saying 'Good' when, really, it wasn't, even if it's easier to lie on the phone because you don't have to look the other person in the eyes.

Later in bed Zachary wondered why looking somebody in the eyes made it more uncomfortable, then remembered his mother had once told him that 'The eyes are the windows to the soul', though he wasn't at all sure what a soul actually was. Unless, he thought, it has something to do with that odd feeling that's creeping up on him recently, the feeling that he's a bit separate from everybody else, is his own person, and not just his parent's son or Tristan's brother or Leo's best friend, but something else, greater.

(Wow. Big thoughts for a kid. And I'm just lying here on the couch eyeing the leftover chips and popcorn on the coffee table waiting for the perfect moment when nobody is looking to steal some! Priorities!)

The next day, the first of a *New* Year (but sadly, Zachary notes, not the end of *Old* Dramas), Mr. and Mrs. Klossner go off to see the new cowboy film, Tristan has invited one of her friends over, and Zachary and Leo are out in the backyard tossing a tennis ball back and forth with Cassia rushing between them in hopes that one will miss—which they sometimes do, being rather clumsy at anything sporty—and then she can grab it in her mouth and race all over the lawn, darting this way and that, while the two boys chase her. She often whams into Lenny the tortoise who is munching on some tall grass along the edge of the lawn that Zachary always misses when it's his turn to mow. Luckily tortoises have super hard shells, so Lenny barely registers the collisions, though he wishes Cassia's PPP was a bit better attuned to Objects In Pathway. Still, it's Cassia's favorite game, and…

(Hold on a sec! Who says it's my 'Favorite Game'? Did I ever stop mid-run and hold up a paw and announce 'Oh, by the way, this is my favorite game'?

It is not, for the record, my favorite game. But #2.

Favorite Game #1 is The Food Toss.

And although there will be those among you who debate whether one can call The Food Toss a game, in my book it is, and at the top of numerous other lists as well:

Favorite Reason To Open My Mouth

Favorite Way To Sample Different Food Varieties

Favorite Bonding Mechanism Between Pet and Owner (cuddling is a close second, I admit)

Favorite Way To Build Front Paw Leaping Muscles

Favorite Method Of Improving Aiming Skills

Favorite Reason To Wake Up In The Morning

Keep this list in mind next time you want to please your dog!)

"Hey, I got an idea," Zachary suddenly says once again yanking the slobbery ball out of Cassia's mouth.

"Yeah, what?" Leo asks, glad to stop and catch his breath.

"Well… Tris and her new friend are right now in the living room, sitting in front of the large sliding glass door, the- clear- glass- door… "

"Oh, Oh, Fake Vomit time!" Leo says excitedly, and they drop the ball and run off towards the house.

(And I am left here on the lawn with Lenny and a ball that he can't throw. So much for 'it's her favorite game'! Lenny's not much good for anything, to be frank, except for the freaky fact that some of his species have been on the earth for one hundred and fifty million years. Oh, and that his top speed is 0.17 miles per hour. See? Now how am I supposed to play chase with THAT?)

Zachary and Leo run through the garage and sneak into the kitchen the back way, peeking in to see that Tristan and her friend in the living room haven't noticed them. Then very quietly they get to work.

It has taken many trials and errors over the years to create the perfect fake vomit—some were too gloppy, others too gloopy, or too runny, or they refused to projectile properly. What they finally settled on was this:

-a bite of a carrot, chewed to small bits

-a spoonful of peanut butter, crunchy is best

-a large spoonful of lime yogurt, for gross green color effect

-a spoonful of raw oats, for texture

Mix all of the above in the mouth until well blended, but still lumpy.

That done, and everything put away, Zachary and Leo sneak back out of the kitchen, through the laundry room, through the garage, and return to the backyard, careful not to let any of the mixture out of their mouths, checking each other on arrival for any dribbles.

Leo gives a thumbs up after checking Zachary's mouth and chin, and Zachary does the same after inspecting Leo's face. Then they proceed with the plan they'd been hatching for weeks, awaiting the perfect opportunity to repeat their great success with another of Tristan's friends last summer.

Fake vomit at correct consistency: Check.

Sister and friend sitting in perfect spot with full view of glass door: Check.

No dribbles: Check

Slowly they then walk to the cement patio, stopping just in front of the glass door where they begin to make squirming gestures of discomfort. Zachary grabs hold of his stomach.

Leo imitates him. Heads slumped over, they move closer towards the door and reach for it as if to grab the handle, when all at once they fling their heads back, quiver, and blast the fake vomit out of their mouths and all over the glass door.

They hear Tristan's friend inside scream.

"Oh my God! Gross! Your brother and his friend are sick, Tris!"

"No, they're not," Tristan says. "They're boys. Trust me, it's not the first time, and won't be the last. PSYCHOS!" she yells the last word at them, but it's too late. They've run off to the garage laughing, bits of greenish goo dribbling down both their chins.

Cassia rushes after them.

(When, really, what I want to be doing is licking the fake vomit up as it puddles at the bottom of the door. Yogurt, peanut butter and oats, yumm!

But I don't, to maintain some sort of dog-dignity.)

CHAPTER 20

The fake vomit episode was the last bit of fun over Christmas vacation, and Zachary dreads getting out of bed the following Monday morning for the first day back at school.

"Zach, down, now. Breakfast is ready," his father calls up the stairs.

"Ugh. Puke. Crap," he groans as he flings the blankets off and goes downstairs in his Scottish plaid pajamas, stopping in the bathroom along the way to pee. On the way out he glances in the mirror and notices a small pimple on his nose.

"Just great," he mumbles to himself.

"It's porridge today," his dad announces as Zachary enters the kitchen. Tristan is already dressed and seated eating hers. Her hair dyed a new color: deep burgundy.

"Raisins or bananas?" Mr. Klossner asks as he serves up a bowl of porridge.

"Burgundy? Really?" Zachary says as he takes a seat staring at Tristan's new hair.

"It's maroon, actually. The color Tibetan monks wear to signify their non-attachment to things," Tristan explains, running a hand through her hair.

"Raisins or bananas?" Mr. Klossner repeats.

"But…um, isn't caring about your hair color, and spending money on the dye, sort of 'attachment'?" Zachary asks as he sips at the orange juice in front of him.

"It's a gesture, Zach. I am making a protest against the way the Tibetans have been suppressed by the Chinese for over half a century."

"Raisins or bananas?"

"Raisins, please," Zachary replies and gulps down the rest of his juice.

"First day back at school, oh boy," Mr. Klossner says as he delivers the bowl to Zachary.

"Yeah. Oh, boy," Zachary mumbles, digging into the porridge, but not feeling very hungry. There are odd sensations in his stomach, and have been since he got his backpack ready for school the night before.

"And you, Dad? You like going back to work after vacation?" Tristan asks between bites. "Even if you did only get four days off."

"Yes, yes, I am glad to be getting back into it. We got a script in just before Christmas, really interesting one, and unique. It's about a sort of teenage outsider, slightly nerdy kid, but sweet, who's befriended by other outsiders, this odd-ball brother and sister, who make him feel…"

"'Perks of Being a Wallflower'," both Tristan and Zachary say in unison.

"Been done already, Dad," Tristan says, widening her eyes and grinning.

"Yeah, pretty good film," Zachary adds. "But Hermione-girl's American accent wasn't so hot."

"It was fine. Dad, really, DONE. And please don't let them do another. I hate it when Holly-wood makes TWO volcano disaster movies at once, or two films on Capote at once. Really! Are they that empty of original ideas?" Tristan says scraping the last porridge out of her bowl.

"Well, maybe you two should write a film script," their Dad replies as he sits down with a bowl of porridge and his 'My Kids Love Me' mug of tea, which was a gift from last Father's Day.

"Painting is my medium, Dad," Tristan replies.

"Yeah, okay, I get that. But what would you write about if you did?"

"I guess mine would be something like 'Frida' or 'Waking Life'—a piece of art as well as a narrative," she answers.

"Hmm. Both interesting films, I agree," their dad says. Sip of tea, then "Zach, what would you write about for a film?"

He sneaks a look over to Tristan, who widens her eyes as if to say 'tell him'.

"About, um…. bullies," Zachary says looking down in his bowl.

"Oh, you mean like 'My Bodyguard' or 'Carrie' or 'Heathers'… "

The telephone rings and he gets up to answer it.

"Oh, and hey, didn't they deal with the bully issue on 'Glee'?" he adds as he picks up the phone. It's a call from work, and he gets into a conversation with his colleague about the script they were contemplating, discussing what works and what doesn't.

"But my kids said it's been done… ," he finally says between listening.

The call goes on and on, and finally Zachary and Tristan need to get going. Teeth need to be brushed. Hair combed. Lunches added to their backpacks.

"And clothes on. Hello!" Tristan says pulling on Zachary's pajamas as they head out the kitchen.

Their dad covers the phone with one hand and turns to them.

"Hey, have a great day back at school. And thanks for the input on the script. I'll convince him to reject it… " Then he's back to the phone conversation. "No that Hermione kid from the 'Harry Potter' films, her, she's in it… "

"Nice try with dad," Tristan says patting Zachary's shoulder as they climb the stairs.

"I was really nervous. Could you tell?" he asks her.

"Other than you nearly dropped your nose into your porridge and I could feel your heartbeat vibrating the tabletop? Mm, no, couldn't tell."

Zachary smiles, and they separate at the top of the stairs, Tristan noticing that he's now nearly her height.

(Meanwhile, if anybody cares, I am under before-mentioned table, and felt the vibrations from Zachary's heartbeat, too. I also felt globs of porridge fall down beside me, but couldn't tell who they came from. And, who cares when it's porridge!

I admit that I spit the raisins out, and in the most hilarious fashion. If only somebody would film me sometime and put it up on YouTube. I'd get a million hits, at least!

'Dogs are miracles with paws' some exceptionally wise human once said. Ain't it the truth!)

CHAPTER 21

Zachary arrives back from school in the late afternoon, calls for Cassia to join him in his room, and before you know it she has a small blue towel tied around her neck that hangs down her back like a cape, and a red rag with two holes cut in it tied across her face like a mask.

(Mio Dio!

That's Italian for 'My God!' In German it's 'Mein Gott!', in French 'Mon Dieu!', and in Dog it's two short yaps followed by one long one. Oops, sidetracked again.

Mio Dio! Zach used to dress me up all the time as various superheroes, but it's been awhile, so I am taken aback when he gets the box labeled 'Costumes' off the top shelf in his closet and puts one on me. It is usually some old towel or fabric for a cape (or in the case of Batman, his old Halloween costume when he was six), and assorted swatches of fabric with eye-holes cut into them for masks—green for Green Hornet, black for Batman, blue for Captain America or red for Superman, like now, though I don't have to heart to tell him that Superman doesn't wear a mask. He seems so troubled today that I just play along with it and pretend.

Eventually Zach flops onto his bed face down and buries his head under his pillow. Naturally I jump up and lie beside him, not easy with the towel tangled up around my paws and a limited view with the stupid mask that's slipping. But I manage, and lie very close to him, snout to cheek, and I can actually feel what he is remembering about his first day back at school. And what I see is this:)

Zachary managed to get to and from his first four classes that morning without any incident. He and Leo met for lunch in their secret hide-away among the trees, both dreading what was to come after lunch: P.E.

But it actually wasn't bad.

First of all, there was a substitute teacher replacing an absent Mr. Parnell —"Hopefully Santa Claus killed him," Leo smirked—but more importantly, being the first day after a long vacation, the boys weren't expected to go immediately into a sport, so they simply suited up and were led through various exercises on the basketball courts--push-ups, running in place, jumping jacks, etc. It happens a few times in a semester, and was always the best day of P.E. for Zachary and Leo—No Team-Picking,

No Competition, No Judgments, No Expectations.

All went well until the showers. After.

It was always a little uncomfortable to undress and shower in front of everybody else, especially as all their bodies were growing and changing differently, and it was hard not to notice.

After you took your shower, you went up to an enclosed cubicle in the middle of the locker room where a student, often one being punished for misbehaving, had the duty to hand out clean towels.

Zachary stood behind two boys already in line as he arrived dripping wet to the cubicle, and as he approached the small window his heart stopped when he saw that it was Joe Padilla assigned to hand out the towels.

Without a word, and not meeting Padilla's eyes, Zachary put out his hand to receive a towel.

"Not until you say a four-letter word, little mama's boy," Padilla demanded, holding back the towel from reach.

Zachary froze. He couldn't bring himself to do it. He knew exactly which of the bad four-letter words Padilla meant—there were at least three he could think of--but it just wasn't him to say them. Especially now, like this, naked and embarrassed and taunted.

"C'mon, little queer boy. Say it!" Padilla demanded, sliding the towel towards him, then quickly pulling it back, and laughing at this.

Zachary could feel his face turn red. He felt so ashamed. And scared. And small. When was this horror ever going to end?

Suddenly he saw his chance when Padilla was distracted, darted his hand out and grabbed the end of the towel with such force that it yanked from Padilla's grip. And Zachary quickly scampered away, knowing that Padilla was stuck in the cage until the class was fully over, and that, for a short while, he was safe.

He dried off and dressed as fast as he could, missing his pant leg numerous times when trying to get his foot through, and leaving one shoe untied. Rushing out of the locker room, he headed for his last class of the day, Biology, arriving in the empty room before anybody else, but at least out of the hallways.

And still quivering.

(And he's quivering again here on the bed as he recalls the day's incident, and I lie here beside him receiving it telepathically. This time it's really bad. I've never

seen Zach so upset before, and doubt that my licks can calm him.

The superhero mask has slipped and totally blocked my eyes, and the towel is all tangled so it's pulling a little at my neck, but I don't mind. My place is right here right now with Zach, doing what we dogs do best: Comfort and befriend.

Unless of course somebody downstairs is eating a bacon sandwich, or even baloney, and calls me for a scrap. Then my allegiance might be tested!)

PART THREE

ELEPHANT REVEALED AND DEALT WITH

CHAPTER 22

A boy had a problem with goons
which often brought feelings of gloom.
It was so big and secret
that he just could not speak it,
like an elephant plopped in the room.

"Pretty good, Zach. But, um... what's with the elephant? What's an elephant got to do with bullies?" Leo asks as he hands the paper back to Zachary and takes a bite from his cheese sandwich, hiding behind tall shrubs in their secret lunch place.

"Ooh, ooh… yuck! Double yuck!" he suddenly groans, grabbing a paper napkin out of his lunch bag and spitting the mouthful of sandwich into it.

"What was it this time?" Zachary asks.

Leo picks up the plastic bag and reads the label that was with the sandwich.

"'Limburger' it says. Oh, disgusting. Smells like dirty socks!"

"Here let me try," Zachary says, and takes a bite. "Yeaaahhh, a bit vile. But my mom raised us on this stuff called Marmite--tastes sorta like concentrated beef broth—so this isn't so bad. Here, I'll have it and you have my peanut butter sandwich." And he hands him his sandwich.

"Oh, god, MUCH better," Leo says taking a bite. Then after he swallows he remembers what they'd been talking about before.

"So wait… um… Elephant… ??" he asks.

"Yeah, well, Tristan said the other day after I'd told her everything about, ya know, at school, that there's this saying, like when there's a problem or something and it's big and right in front of everybody but nobody wants to talk about it, so it's like there's a HUGE elephant right there standing in the middle of the room and everybody is trying to ignore it."

"Yeah, okay," Leo says after another bite from his/Zach's sandwich. "But…. why an elephant? Why not a Rhinoceros in the room, or Dinosaur in the room? Or, hey, what about a Mountain in the room?"

"Mountain? Where'd you come up with that?"

"My dad's always saying 'Don't make a mountain out of a molehill', so I thought we could, you know, connect the two. Like, um…. 'Don't make an elephant out of a molehill'. Or, or, 'Don't make a mountain out of an elephant in the room'."

"Doesn't quite make sense, Leo."

"Okay, but I still don't see why bullies at school are like an elephant in the room."

"Because the bullying is so big and so obvious and everybody is pretending that nothing's happening."

"Yeah, but The Elephant part??"

"Forget the elephant. It's just a saying."

Leo takes another bite from the sandwich, thinking for a minute.

"Okay, so what do we do? Break down a wall and let the Elephant out of the room?" he asks. "Or shoot it?"

"Shoot it??"

"Yeah, you know, like on Animal Planet. Those guys who shoot elephants for their nose bone thingies."

"I think you mean tusks, and it's illegal."

"So help me out here… what do we do with our elephant?" Leo asks again.

"Well… we turn around and face it first of all. And then force everybody else to."

"And how do we do that?" Leo asks, reaching into his lunch bag for the usual apple and finding a plum.

"I don't know. Tris says we start by telling people that it's happening. Like a teacher or something."

"Yeah, right! Half the teachers let it happen! I mean, my English teacher, Mr. Shamony, hears kids calling each other names all the time, and all he does is correct their grammar!"

"I know somebody here at a school who might help," Zachary says as he reaches into his pocket and takes out a piece of paper folded up. He opens it and reads from it. "I, um, Googled 'Bullies' and it said 'A bully is somebody who taunts or hurts…'"

"Wait. Tante's your great aunt. She's not a bully… "

"No, taunt, t-a-u-n-t. It means, like, to pick on." He reads again. "A bully is somebody who taunts or hurts other people for their own pleasure'. Another site said that a bully is a person who takes out their anger on other people."

"Huh, that's for sure," Leo smirks. "But I'm tired of being their punching bag. Their dartboard. Their spittoon."

"Spittoon?"

"Yeah, my grandpa chews tobacco and he spits it into this brass pot thing called a spittoon," Leo explains.

"Yuck. You mean i*n the house?*"

"Yeah, right by his chair. Often he misses, but grandma always cleans it up without saying anything."

"Gross," Zach replies, biting into a cookie. "Hey, has anybody ever spit on you here at school?"

"Sure, lots of times… but, I don't wanna talk about it, Zach. It makes me feel bad again."

"Yeah, I know. Me, too. But if we don't talk about it… I mean, who CAN we talk about it with?"

"Well… true. So, like, many times I've been spit on, yeah. And somebody flicked a cigarette butt at me from the school bus window. Another time a guy threw bits of his macaroni and cheese across the table at me in the cafeteria. That's before I stopped eating there… "

(Really? They do that in the school cafeteria: throw food that lands on the floor wasted?? Might I suggest

they allow kids to bring their pet dogs with them to school to help clean up the cafeteria floor. I'd volunteer!

By the way as I lie here alone on Zachary's bed pretending to be totally asleep, I have my psychic ears open and can decipher everything they say. And I must acknowledge that I am proud of Leo for not suggesting 'A dog in the room', as it would be rather insulting, for unlike elephants, we are far too adorable to be right smack in the middle of a room full of people and IG-NORED. Would never happen!)

They both finish up their lunch quickly when they hear the bell announcing the next class period. Leo stands up, peering through the trees out at the open quad, hesitant to move.

"It's called Agoraphobia," Zachary says.

"What is?"

"Fear of open places."

"It's not the open space I am afraid of. It's what might be lurking in it!"

CHAPTER 23

The next day when he should be heading off to PE class, Zachary instead paces and back and forth in a small corridor where few students pass. He has a sudden urge to pee, but knows it's not safe, as tough kids often hang out in the bathrooms between classes, smoking, swearing, and picking on anything smaller than them.

"Can't go to class. Can't go to pee. That's it!" he mumbles to himself, then moves along the less crowded corridors, bypassing any open areas, until he arrives at the Administrative building, where he moves quickly down the wood-paneled hallway, past the Faculty Office and Faculty Lounge, goes into the small bathroom to pee, then past the Principal's and Vice Principal's offices, and taps lightly on the door of the Nurse.

Mrs. Wells beckons him in and directs him to sit on the patient bed while she inventories new medications at her desk, her reading glasses strung around her neck with red plastic string.

"What is it this time, Zachary? Headache? Stomachache? Sore throat?"

"None of them," he replies. "It's an elephant."

"Oh, that's original. Stuck in your throat or your stomach?" she says, smiling.

"Mrs. Wells, I'm not sick. I never really was whenever I came in here. I mean, I feel sick, which is why I come in, but… but it's not a sickness because of head or throat or whatever."

She realizes the serious tone and turns around in her chair, leaning towards him, dropping her glasses off and looking him in the eyes.

"Go on, Zachary, I'm listening."

"I feel sick inside because… here at school, in P.E. especially, the other boys they… "

"They what, Zachary?"

"It's Zach, remember."

"Yes, sorry. Go on, Zach."

"Well, they… pick on me… ," he says as his eyes start to water. He tries not to let them, but they do anyway, and he is so tired of trying to stop them, that he just let's go, and so do the tears.

"Do they pick on you... all the time?"

"Not all the time," he says through his tears, "but a lot. Too much. And it hurts too bad."

"Are you talking about being bullied?" she asks, wanting to be sure.

Zachary looks down at the floor and lightly nods.

"Zachary...Zach, lots of kids over the years here at Middle School get bullied, and some say it's part of growing up... "

He glances up and looks her in the eyes.

"If that's true, it's the horrible part!"

"... but I don't agree with that, not at all. I think bullying is intolerable."

"What's that?"

"Intolerable: not to be tolerated or allowed. Much of bullying may be harmless teasing and such, but some of it can be very harmful. Mean. Even dangerous. And I've been trying for a long time to get the school committee to address the issue of Bullying. You coming here today now makes me want to push harder. For you and the others."

"Lots of others! I see it happening all the time to other kids... ," Zachary says.

"Listen, Zach. I'm going to bring this up with the principal at a meeting this Friday. Can you put up with P.E. a little longer?"

"I don't think so. I don't want to. It's awful."

"Right. Well… ,"she says spinning around in her chair and facing her desk. Putting her glasses back on she reaches for a notepad and begins writing on it.

"I'm writing you an excuse to be exempt from any more P.E. classes for the time being…we'll say you get headaches from running or something."

"Thank you," Zachary says meekly, wiping his tears on his shirt sleeve.

"…and we'll get this sorted out, promise," she adds as she rips the note off the pad and spins the chair back around, holding it out to Zachary. He puts up his hand and takes it.

"You bring that to Mr. Parnell. If he has any questions, he can come to me."

"He watches it, ya know."

"He watches what, Zach? Who?"

"Mr. Parnell, he sees the bullies do it and doesn't try to stop it. He, like, picks the tough kids to be captain knowing they'll leave some boys until last…it happens all the time. And in the locker room… "

"What happens in the locker room?"

"It's even worse. The smaller kids, or the weak, shy ones, get hit and called names, and a friend of mine was locked up in a locker. I saw this Muslim kid named Moula beat up in the showers...his nose was bleeding and they called him horrible things... "

"Oh, I'm truly sorry to hear that," the nurse says, dropping her head down.

"Listen, Zach, I must ask you. Were you ever beaten up?" she then asks.

"You mean, like, fist in face? No... not really," he says. "But that doesn't mean they didn't hurt me."

"Yes, you're right. Listen, Zach, you're a brave young man to come in here and tell me all this. Very brave. These bullies are not brave. They are weak, inside, that's why they pick on kids weaker than they are, because it makes them feel strong, because they are not."

"When they push me around they feel pretty strong!"

"Zach, do you know what 'Overcompensation' means?"

"Umm... I don't think so."

"It's when somebody does something to cover up opposite things going on inside of them. Like, well, you know all those priests who are supposed to be more pure than the rest of us, how they got caught doing really bad things? So people often became priests precisely to *show* a cover of Purity to mask their bad thoughts. See what I mean?"

"I think I do. So like all those celebrities on Oprah who say they became big and famous because they always felt insecure and unloved?"

"Yes, that's right. We think of them as together and confident, but actually, with many of them it's the opposite. They are overcompensating. See, Zach, it's the same with people who bully. I know it might be hard to understand, but many of them were probably bullied themselves, so they feel small and weak, and they overcompensate by acting tough. They pick on weaker people to feel better about themselves."

"That's sad."

"It is sad, yes. If you can try and think of that when you see them, instead of just fear, you might feel sorry for them, too."

"I can't feel that right now… "

"I understand. Just think about it." And she stands up. "You go give that to Mr. Parnell at some point before your next P.E. class, and leave me to work out the rest. And I may need you to assist me on this."

"Assist you? How… ?"

"Well, you've told me here what I've suspected for a long time about a lot of kids who come in here with supposed illnesses. I'm ashamed I didn't follow my feelings more and investigate it. But some people might not believe that it's so bad, so I might need you to tell your story to others."

"I don't know if… I mean, if the other kids find out, you know… they'll beat me up or something."

"It will all be confidential, Zach."

"But I'm not confident!"

"No, dear, 'confidential'. It means that it will all be kept secret. None of the other kids will know you spoke out. Don't worry."

Zachary gets up and hesitantly crosses the room towards the door. He really doesn't want to leave this space, her office. It feels so safe.

"Can't I stay here until P.E. is out?" he asks.

"Well, I've got a 2:30 appointment coming in… um, you can go in the Faculty Office and help out with the weekly newsletter or making copies or something. Tell them I sent you."

"Oh, great. Thanks."

"Thank YOU, Zachary. I mean, Zach."

(I'm sniffling here on the kitchen floor. Poor Zach! But I'm glad he finally told somebody besides me. I mean, what am I supposed to do with all those confessions and secrets besides lick his face or try to get him to play tug-of-war with a pair of socks to distract him? I thought of going to find the bullies and biting them because some humans said 'An eye for an eye, a tooth for a tooth'. But then another human said 'Turn the other cheek' when you get offended, which I interpret as 'snout', and think that's a better policy.

Besides which I have a major distaste for human flesh. You guys taste icky.)

CHAPTER 24

At the weekend Mr. Klossner takes Zachary and Leo to see the new superhero movie. (At first he suggested they go see a film called 'Middle School: The Worst Years Of My Life', but both boys at once immediately said "NO!")

As always, they discuss it in the car afterwards, and all agree that there were too many special effects, and that it just gets boring after a while.

"But I like his cool costume, and that cycle he rode. I want one!" Leo adds as they come to a stoplight.

Zachary turns to Leo in the back seat, winks and says "Get ready... ," and then puts his head out the open window and makes a very loud screeching monkey call, and the boys quickly duck down so when all the drivers and pedestrians look at the source of the shrill noise, all they see is Mr. Klossner alone in the car.

"Cute, Zach. Nice one," Mr. Klossner smiles, waving to all the drivers glancing over at him.

"You've been doing that since you were, what, five years old?"

"Six," he answers lying down scrunched on his seat, smiling. Leo is giggling in the back.

The light eventually changes to green, and Mr. Klossner drives on, a few people on the sidewalk still staring at him. Knowing something has been bothering his son for a while, but not sure how to bring the subject up, he offers to take the boys to their favorite ice cream place.

"GELATO!" they both yell at once, popping back up in their seats. They drive a few blocks over and park in a small shopping mall.

Leo orders Mint Chip for his two scoops, "Like always," Zachary remarks, and he tries a new flavor combination, one of Pineapple and one of Coconut.

"Ooh, a Pina Colada," his dad says.

"A what?" Zach asks.

"Never mind. Later," Mr. Klossner says, and Zachary figures it must be one of those Adult Things that parents keep secret, thinking kids aren't ready to hear.

His dad orders a scoop of Killer Coffee and one of Dangerously Dark Chocolate in a cup instead of cone.

They sit at a table in the back of the shop, where lining the walls are framed black and white photographs of places in Italy--the Grand Canal in Venice, the Duomo of Florence, the Roman Coliseum. The white plastic tabletop is dirty with gelato plops and puddles from the previous customers, so they scoot over to the next table.

"Dad, tell us one of the lame scripts you had to read last week," Zachary says licking up a large melting bit of coconut ready to drop down his cone.

"Did I tell you the one about the kid who switches roles with the adult?"

Leo smacks his head. "Not again!"

"Yeah Dad, c'mon, " Zach smirks. " 'Big', '17 Again', 'Freaky Friday'....."

"TWO versions!" Leo adds.

"It's been done enough. Seriously, Dad!"

"Wait, now wait, hear me out," Mr. Klossner says swallowing a luscious gulp of his Dangerous Dark Chocolate gelato. "Yes, it's been done with a *human* kid and adult, but this one's about a *zombie* kid and his zombie dad!"

"Jeez. Seriously? Sounds double lame, Dad."

"You're right. It was pretty lame. And the studio wanted to commission it as musical. You know, 'Chicago' and 'Les Miz' made musicals hip again."

Leo nearly spits up a mouthful of gelato from his giggling. Recovering he says, "A musical? Singing and dancing zombies??"

"Like Bullywood!" Zach nudges Leo. "Remember that Indian film we saw where their mouths didn't even match their singing. And those crazy fight scenes?"

"Yeah, that was soooo lame!"

"Hey, Dad," Zachary then asks, "Is it called Bullywood because everybody's always getting beaten up in them?"

"Ha! No, son. It's BOLLYwood, not Bullywood. They're mostly from Bombay, so it's a play on the word Hollywood."

"And what's that a play on, Dad? I heard there was no holly wood in the area?"

"Beats me. I'll have to look that up," Mr. Klossner says.

(A tabletop with multiple blotches of gelato spills and I'm not there to lick them up? What a waste!

Meanwhile, Tristan and I are at home on the couch watching some Celebrity News on TV, and they just announced that the rapper Snoop Dogg's real name is Calvin Broadost. More name changes.

But if you ask me, Snoop Dogg is a big improvement over Calvin. Just saying.)

When they finish up and drive back to the Klossner home, Leo decides to stay over a little, and he and Zachary go up to his room. Cassia jumps off the couch and follows, sniffing at both boys' clothes.

(Well, YEAH! Gelato spills. HELLO!)

The boys collapse on the floor and lie down looking up at the ceiling, their bellies full from too much popcorn at the movie and the gelato afterwards. Zachary burps, and though Leo tries to get one to come out, he can't.

"Hey, I thought you were about to tell your dad about school and stuff," Leo then says as Cassia licks at a Mint Chip stain on his pant leg.

"Cassia, stop!" he says. She moves over to Zachary, sniffs around, and finds where a drop of Pineapple gelato fell near his knee and begins licking at it.

"I was ready to tell him. I mean, I almost did, but then… I don't know. He's always so… happy about things, and I didn't want to make him upset," Zachary says staring up at the ceiling. Then, "Cassia, please!" and he pushes her head away from his pant leg which she's dampened with all her licking. "Go lie down!" he says pointing to his bed.

(All right already. Jeez, guys, I'm just trying to help by cleaning the stains on your pants for you.)

"Did you tell your mom yet?" Leo asks.

Zachary shakes his head.

"But Tris knows… some of it. She saw it at the mall, after all. Hey! Look up there! See the face in the ceiling?" Zachary says pointing overhead to a particular spot.

"I couldn't tell my parents, ever," Leo says, trying to see the face Zach's pointing out. "They'd say it was my fault or something. I mean, my dad thinks I'm not macho enough already. He always tried to get me to play catch when I was little, but I didn't care about it like he does. Gordon did… "

"Yeah, but you guys go fishing together a lot."

"I love fishing! Well, not the gutting-the-fish part… "

Cassia's one-and-a-half ears twitch.

(Fish guts? Did I hear Fish Guts??)

"Maybe the nurse can really do something about it… ," Zachary ponders.

"She better. I can't put up with this all semester, and then in ninth grade, too!" Leo
says, then adds, "I wonder if it goes on in high
school? Oh god, then THREE more years. I'd
rather die… "

"Tris says it gets better in high school."

"How would she know? She's a girl."

"Girls get bullied, too. Especially on Facebook and stuff. Well, I mean, SHE did. She
says the other girls made fun of her because
she wasn't into wearing make-up and the new
fashions and all that."

"Oh, yeah, *now* I see the face," Leo suddenly announces. "Oh, wow, it looks like an old
man. And, look! There's a cloud!"

"There are lots of clouds. Almost every
plaster bit looks like a cloud," Zachary says
glancing all over the ceiling.

"Yeah, but that one *really* looks like a cloud!"

"Anyhow, so, yeah, Tris says there's less bullying in high school."

"Thank god!"

*(What god is Leo thanking, I wonder? A Hindu
god, a Pagan god, the Muslim god, the Christian god?
There are so many gods throughout your human history!*

*Me, I thank the Gelato God, because I've got Mint
Chip flavor on my lips now and I can sleep happily.*

Hey! I wonder if they make Fish Gut gelato?? Mmm mm!)

CHAPTER 25

Because Leo mentioned Tante a couple days ago, Zachary's been thinking a lot about her, and figures that maybe she'd be a good one to get advice about the bullying.

So on Saturday morning he calls her and asks if he can come over.

He knows what bus to take to her place because he's gone over a few times before on his own. Like when she sprained her ankle last spring tripping in her garden, and he went over every other day after school for two weeks to wash her dishes and make her tea. Sometimes Tristan would go too, and they'd clean her house together, Tristan dusting off all the furniture and Zachary vacuuming up afterwards. Then Tante would call out for a pizza or Indian or Middle-Eastern food to be delivered for an early dinner. Zachary always preferred the pizza, but he was getting more and more used to the odd foreign food Tante was introducing him to.

One afternoon when they arrived, she had all the ingredients out on the counter by the stove for the kids to make Indian Chai instead of just the usual English tea with milk and sugar separate. Following Tante's hand-written recipe they put the black tea powder in a pot of half-water and half-milk, added some ginger and cinnamon and some weird crushed pods, then a little sugar, and let the whole thing boil. When it became a nice coppery brown color, they poured it through a small strainer into three glasses.

"It's really good," Zachary commented after his first sip. Tristan agreed.

"But why in glasses and not teacups?" he asked.

Tante explained that she saw Indians making chai on a TV documentary, and all over India they often drank it in small glasses.

"I wrote down the recipe from the program and make it whenever I want a full, hearty tea. 'Chai' is simply the Hindu word for 'Tea', which the British discovered in China centuries ago and made the locals grow it for them when they settled in India. When it's got all these spices in it, it's called a 'Masala Chai'."

"So, wait. If 'chai' means tea, and it always has milk", Tristan asked, "why do cafes here call it 'Chai Tea Latte'? That's like saying 'Chai Chai Chai'!"

"This is America, Tris. We don't always make sense", was all Tante had said, but it made Zachary think that she really thinks quite differently from what's normal. Although she's always been thought of as sort of zany and eccentric, maybe it was a cover for feeling unusual and different.

So that's why he chose her as the first adult in the family to tell about the Bullying.

He arrives in the late morning on Saturday, walking the two blocks from the local bus stop to her house, a one-story from the 1920's, white with deep green trim and a high-pitched roof like a temple.

The smell of her house when she opens the door soothes him at once. And just as he guessed, there is a pot of Indian chai and two glasses awaiting him on the coffee table. Nearby is a plate of chocolate chip cookies, still warm and gooey when he grabs the first one off the plate and takes a large bite.

"If there *is* a Heaven, it would be wall-to-wall chocolate chip cookies," he says as he gobbles the cookie and then takes a sip from the smooth spicy chai Tante had poured for him after a long welcoming hug.

"Oh, I think so, too," Tante smiles. "IF there is a Heaven."

"You don't think there is?" Zachary asks.

"Oh, I don't know, honey. None of us KNOWS, in fact. They're all just stories people have been telling each other for centuries now-- God, the Devil, Heaven, Hell." And she rises from her chair and grabs a cookie for herself.

"So you don't think people can be good or bad. I mean, like evil?"

Tante starts giggling at Zachary.

"Dumb question?" he asks shyly, always on edge about being picked on.

"No, no, dear, a very *good* question. But, um…. there's a huge blotch of melted chocolate on your upper lip and it makes you look like Hitler. So it's funny with that, and then you asking about good and evil."

Zachary licks his upper lip, and it takes a few pass-overs with the tongue to get all the chocolate off.

"Better?" he shows Tante his face.

"Yes. Now, have another cookie and I'll try to answer your question as best I can. You see, Zach, probably, really *everybody* has both good and evil in them. We are capable of lovely kind gestures—like you coming over to help me when I hurt my ankle. You didn't have to. Nobody forced you. And we all do some evil acts, however small. Remember how you and Leo used to sprinkle salt on snails and watch them fizzle up and die? Well, okay, you were little. But, you see what I mean?"

"And people like Hitler?" Zach asks. "In our History class we studied the Second World War, with the Holocaust and all that. It was pretty awful."

"Yes, it was truly horrific what people did to each other. We had relatives back in Germany and they had to flee into Switzerland. Many weren't so fortunate."

"So, what… are we Jewish?"

"No, not really. Well, I mean there's talk that we've got maybe a little bit of Jewish blood. Some Arab, too. You know, all Americans are a big mix of lots of ethnicities. A grand masala, like this chai." And she takes a sip from her glass.

"Besides which, it wasn't only Jews who were exterminated, Zach. They killed anybody who was different—gypsies, homosexuals, Communists, the handicapped."

"I'd call that evil… "

"Yes. But did you know that when Hitler was young he wanted to be an artist? A great artist?"

"No way! Seriously? You mean like Tris?"

"Yes, just like Tris. It didn't go so well, so he studied instead to be an architect. I know it's not politically correct to say such things, but you see, Zach, he just shifted his energies from Creating to Destroying, its opposite. He had them both inside. Perhaps if he'd succeeded in Art none of the Holocaust would have happened, who knows? Or maybe somebody else would have initiated it."

"So… if nobody is really just bad, what makes somebody become like that? I mean, to hurt people?"

"Well, I suppose when people become so horrible something must have been terribly off in their head. Probably some bad experience from his childhood, that's almost always the case for later problems. I read that young Adolf and his older brother were treated brutally by their father, Zach. And when such people grow up they often take their own inner anger and frustration out on other people."

Zachary looks down into his Masala Chai.

"That's just what Mrs. Wells said," he mumbles.

"I'm sorry, what, Zach? Who's Mrs. Wells?"

"She's the nurse at school. I… I've been seeing her a lot this year."

"And why is that? You okay, Zach?" she asks, concerned.

"Physically, yes. Nothing to do with that, Tante." Then, scared to follow through, he asks, "Can I have another cookie?"

"Of course. And what you don't finish you take home. So, I'm sorry, I'm confused, honey. If nothing's wrong physically, why do you keep going to see the nurse at school?"

Zachary keeps his glance into his chai glass, but he can feel a heavy presence suddenly in the room. It was the elephant. And it was demanding to be addressed.

"Tante, I… ," he starts to say. Tante notices the sudden seriousness in his face, puts her glass down on the side table by her chair, and moves over to the couch and sits alongside him. She grabs his free hand.

"Zachary Bartholomew Klossner, you know you can talk to me about anything. I'm here, honey."

Water starts to fill his eyes and he looks up at her.

"ANYTHING, Zach."

"At school… some of the kids, other boys… they're mean."

"Mean to you?"

Zachary nods, his face dropping back down towards his chai.

"Take a drink, Zach, slow and calm. Then turn and look at me and just say it. No fear. No judgment. I want to know."

He does as she says, takes a sip from the chai, but he almost feels nauseous when it goes down. So he takes a deep breath and slowly, very slowly, turns to look at Tante. Her eyes are warm and glowing, and he knows that every thought and consideration he's ever had, and will ever have, is safe in her presence.

"I'm getting bullied at school, Tante," he lets out.

Suddenly the elephant stomps its foot and roars.

"A lot," he adds. "Leo, too. Many kids are. It hurts and I don't know how to stop it."

And tears come streaming out, and he doesn't try to block them. He buries his head in Tante's lap and lets them flow.

The elephant is smiling.

'Finally!' it seems to say.

(*'Finally!' I do say, lying here on Zach's bed while he takes this all-important mission to his Tante. I've got my head on his pillow to connect more deeply with him, and I can feel a great release come out of him. I'm so proud of him for facing up to what's happening. And, not to be disrespectful to the critical nature of the situation, but I do hope he brings home some left-over chocolate chip cookies, because I know he'll give me a whole one for sure!*

Side Note: Although you humans are suddenly over-ly-concerned about feeding chocolate to dogs, honestly, Google it, folks. It is only a few rare breeds that a LOT of chocolate could possibly do harm to.

We Unique Blend dogs can handle anything in moderation.

So bring on the cookies!)

CHAPTER 26

Tante comes out from the kitchen and back into her living room with their glasses of chai refilled halfway.

"Sorry, that's all that's left," she says as she hands Zachary his glass, then sits down beside him on the couch. She looks at him for a moment, wondering what to say.

"You know, Zach, I was thinking. Have you tried just not reacting at all to the bullies? Because sometimes they'll eventually ignore you if they don't get the satisfaction out of seeing you get upset."

He shakes his head lightly and takes a sip of chai.

"Mm. Even better now," he says pulling the glass away from his mouth.

"Yes. The spices have had time to stew and release all their fragrance."

"Yummy umm."

"So just keep in mind, Zach: bullies feel bad inside, but can't bear it, so they try to make others feel worse than they do, so they can feel higher. I know… ," she says pulling his face up to look at him. "I was bullied, too, Zach."

"You? You mean they had bullies way back then?"

"Oh, gosh. There have been people bullying people for centuries, dear—individuals, religions, groups, ethnicities, nations. Those men who flew airplanes into buildings in New York were bullying us. And what was our response? Go bully back! And look where that got us to."

"I would never… could never bully them back!" Zachary says.

"Not now. But if it kept going on for years, you might get so frustrated that you then go out looking for weaker people that you could bully, to feel better. Most of those kids who shoot other students at school, they were bullied. See how it works?"

"I guess so. But, I mean, okay, the bullies are feeling bad inside, too. But that doesn't help *me*!"

"No, you're right. It doesn't. It's not correct what they are doing, and the problem must be addressed, absolutely. Have you told anyone at school?"

"Yes. The nurse. She's a nice lady and said she'd bring it up at some meeting or something."

"Good. That's a start. Let's see where it leads. Meanwhile, you need to tell your parents, Zachary. I assume you haven't… "

He shakes his head.

"Honey, you must. They should know what you're going through. Maybe they can't stop it, but at least they can be there and fully support you at home. And they will. Your parents are good people, Zach. Both of them."

Zachary puts his empty glass down and gets up.

"I better go… "

"Of course. Thanks for confiding in me."

"I did *what* in you?" he asks.

"Confided. Trusted me to tell your secret. And I won't say a word to your parents. It's up to you to tell them when the time's right. But… before you go, might I ask a wonderful and brave young man to help me put the Christmas decoration boxes back up in the attic? They've been sitting on the floor waiting there for weeks now."

"Sure, Tante."

She gets a small step-ladder from the narrow space between her frig and the wall that Zachary takes and carries to the hallway, just below the covered hole in the ceiling. He climbs up, pops the cover up and over, and places the boxes, which she hands up to him, off to one side in the attic.

"Ooh, creepy up here," he says with his head in the darkness. "It'd make a great hide-out!"

"Except that if you go beyond that piece of plywood where the boxes are," she replies, "you'd crash right through the ceiling below. Fun over!"

Their good-bye hug at the door lingers. He doesn't really want to leave there… ever! And she wishes there was some way to ease his pain, but is aware that as he grows out of childhood and becomes an adult, the world will be a challenging place for him, and he will have to learn to maneuver his way.

He thanks her again, and she thanks *him* again, and he runs off—there is a bus in eight minutes he can catch if he hurries.

It comes by just as he arrives to the corner, breathless he jumps on it, but gets off one stop before the one closest to his house, because it's a block from Leo's, where he decides to go next.

"Great! Come in!" Leo says when he answers the door and unexpectedly finds Zachary.

"I thought of some more crazy English," he says as they head out the back door towards the treehouse.

"Oh, wait a sec," Leo says, and rushes back to the kitchen, returning with half a bag of B-B-Q chips.

When they are up in the treehouse munching on chips, orange-red powder covering their fingers, chin and lips, Leo tells Zachary his new revelation about the English language.

"How do you spell cough?" he asks.

"C-O-U-G-H," Zach answers. "And?"

"And you pronounce it like 'Coff', right? So how do you pronounce R-O-U-G-H?"

"Like 'Ruff'." Zach replies. "Oh, yeah. Weird."

"Wait, it gets weirder," Leo says stuffing a huge curled chip in his mouth. "Ooh, like those ones best," he smiles, B-B-Q powder on the tip of his nose.

" So… how do you pronounce T-H-R-O-U-G-H?" he then asks.

"Um, like 'Throo'."

"And D-O-U-G-H?"

"Ah... like 'Doe'. God, that is crazy. Four sounds for the same spelling and none of them sounds like how it's spelled..."

... "which should be... 'Doe-U-Gaha'."

"Gosh I never thought of it... oh, wait! Thought, T-H-O-U-G-H-T, sounds like 'Thot'."

"So that's FIVE different ways to say it! Pretty lame, no?"

"Yeah, really!" Zach says.

"So where'd you guys go this morning? I called twice but nobody was at home," Leo asks him digging his hand down deep into the almost-empty chips bag. When he pulls it up he's got only a few crumbs, but all his fingers are covered in orange-red powder.

"I don't know where everybody else is, but I went to go see my Tante. I think they may-be went to a movie, that new rom-com with what's-her-face," Zachary says as he's brushing his hands together to remove the B-B-Q powder.

"Eww, her. She reminds me of Gretchen in our Biology class."

"Gretchen Montgomery? No way. She's way better looking than big-nose Gretchen!"

"Is not!" Leo says poking Zachary in the ribs.

"Is so!" Zachary pokes him back and Leo spits a spray of orange-red bits. So Zachary leaps over and pins the smaller Leo down and blows on his face.

"Say that actress is cuter. Say it!"

"Hey, get off! You're hurting my arm!" Leo says, almost laughing.

"Say it. C'mon!" Zachary insists.

"Get off you bully!" Leo yells, which stuns Zachary and he lets go and sets Leo free.

They stare at each other a moment, both suddenly aware of what just took place. And worse, that Zachary had just referred to a girl at school as Big Nose, just like the bullies do.

Suddenly they hear a splintering CRACK in a floorboard. Leo scoots quickly out of the way just in time as one of the old narrow boards breaks away, falling down in two jagged pieces, leaving a hole in the floor that they could fit one foot through.

"That was close!" Leo remarks.

"Good thing we found out now. Imagine if we'd brought Gwendolyn or Cassia up again and they fell through. Instant Dog Mush!"

(Not a pretty picture. And, actually, I have only been up there once and wouldn't go again-- I came home with wood splinters in my sensitive paw pads. And if truth be told, I'm a little bit scared of heights. Acrophobia, Zach says it's called. Yes, yes, I know—it's my ONE fault.)

The boys climb down and find another piece of wood from a stack of old lumber back behind the house. They put the two pieces of the broken board together to measure the exact length, mark it on the new piece, and use a hand saw to cut the new piece to fit. Leo has to go back in the garage for a hammer and some nails, and spots a small pulley, then some rope, and after replacing the floor board they develop a pulley system to bring a bucket up and down for carrying food or supplies or whatever.

"What I'd really wish is that we could get electricity up here," Zach says after they test the pulley by loading Gwendolyn in the basket and pulling her up, and then back down again. Before the basket even touches the ground she leaps out and rushes off.

"Oh, hey! My dad put in an outdoor light before Christmas and it has a socket on it," Leo says. "So if we get an extension chord we

can plug it in and bring it up here, and PRES-
TO! Electricity!"

"Think it's okay if we do that?" Zach asks.

"Sure. My dad let's me use his tools, just not
the electric ones, but all the others. He thinks
that's what makes a man. C'mon!" And they
start to climb down the tree.

"Really? Playing with tools makes you a
man?" Zach comments on the way down.
"Tris plays with my dad's tools, so what does
that make *her*?"

"I dunno… "

"And my dad hardly touches his tools, so
what does that make *him*?"

"Stupid rule. Who wrote it anyway?" Leo
says as they make the final leap from the lowest
branch onto the ground.

"I don't think it *is* written. That's what
makes it so stupid. And who cares, anyway?"
And Zachary takes off, running across the
back lawn to the side garage door, Leo just behind him.

They spend the rest of the afternoon hook-
ing up electricity to the treehouse and plug-
ging in an old desk lamp they find in the garage. When they are rummaging through all
the storage cabinets they spot an old carpet,

torn at one corner and faded, and after Zachary sweeps out the treehouse of all the leafy bits and B-B-Q chip crumbs, they roll out the carpet and set the lamp on a small table. Leo goes down and comes back with two cans of fruit juice that he puts in the basket and brings them up with the new pulley system. Zachary then remembers the bag of Tante's cookies in his backpack, pulls them out, and they hang out until the sun gets very low and the sky begins to darken a little and Zachary walks the few blocks home.

"Oh, Zach, you missed the film," his mother greets him when he walks in.

She's flopped on the couch, with her left hand cuddling Vermeer and her right hand cuddling Dali, who's got one back leg up and over his head, licking his thigh for a bath.

"I missed it on purpose, Mom," Zachary replies as he sits alongside her and pats Vermeer's soft belly. He begins to purr loudly.

"Yeah, well, it *was* sort of a chick flick," she admits. "So how was your visit with Tante? She doing okay? You there all day?"

"It was good. She's well. And, no, I left there about one and hung out at Leo's all afternoon. Hey, where's Cassia?"

"Up with your sister. Sitting for another portrait, I believe."

Zachary leans down and kisses both cats, and then heads up the stairs and peeks in Tristan's open door.

Cassia immediately looks over at him with an imploring look. She is sitting upright on the bed surrounded by many cushions, and she is all wrapped up in various fabrics—one over her shoulders like a shawl, another wrapped around her waist like a skirt, a couple of scarves over her head, one wrapped as a turban. Her tail wags when she sees Zach looking at her and the fabric around her waist starts to unravel.

"Cassia, hold still!" Tristan yells. "Zach, look what you've done. Calm her down, will ya? She listens to you."

"Cassia stay," he says. "Stay… " Then crosses over to pat her head. Her scarfed and turbaned head.

"Um, what's she supposed to be?" Zach asks as he walks behind Tristan and looks at what she is painting with watercolors.

"The assignment was Ethnicity, so I'm doing a Gypsy," she replies, the paintbrush adding blackness to Cassia's nostrils.

"A gypsy *dog*, you mean," Zachary smirks.

"The statement didn't specify species."

(Oh cute—'Specify Species'. Does she think that some clever alliteration makes up for my humiliation?

Okay, what about 'Humiliating Human Hubris'.

Or, or, 'Cultivating Canine Contempt'.

Oh, oh, I got one.

'Anarchist Artist Abuses Adorable Animal'!)

Zachary shakes his head and turns around to leave.

'Good Luck, Tris. You, too, Cassia," he says and walks out the door.

(Sure. Right, buddy. Leave without saving me from my shame.

Okay, Zach. I got one for you now... um, um... darn! I can't think of any other words that start with a 'Z'!)

CHAPTER 27

"A pale young slender and sensitive boy dis-
covers that he comes from a long line of Dru-
ids, and for one night a year at the Summer
Solstice he possesses magical powers where he
can do whatever he wishes—go anywhere, see
anybody, make anything happen. So he decides to try and Right All Wrong in the world,
until he comes to realize that his father robs
money from customers at the bank where he
works and his older brother sells illegal weap-
ons to terrorists… "

"What, no psycho sister who dismembers
animals?" Tristan says when her father finishes
telling his kids over breakfast about the script
he read the day before.

"What, no big battle at the end between
Good and Evil?" Zachary adds, then spoons in
another bite of porridge.

*(And what, no side-kick Druid dog to assist slender
sensitive boy in righting all wrong? I'd rather be a superhero dog and wear a cape and mask than all those*

silly scarves, portrait posing for two and half hours! Without a pee break!)

"Dad, let me ask you," Tristan continues. "Have you ever dealt with a film at work that was *not* like major lame?"

"Not major lame… ? Hmm," he ponders. "Nope!"

"Hey, at least we get in free to see movies," Zach interjects.

"That is a major perk, yes," their dad agrees. "And, hey, I don't take it so seriously. I'm not there to make Art. I leave that undertaking to you kids."

"Both of us? No way. Tris is the artist in the family," Zach responds.

"Mm, maybe up 'til now. But I think that you, Zachary Bartholomew Klossner have some secrets up your sleeves."

"Um, first, that's the second time somebody's called me by my full name recently, dorky middle name included," Zach says putting down his porridge spoon. "And number two, I'd hardly call writing Limericks an Art."

"True on both counts," his father says sitting down at the table with his bowl of porridge. "But I think maybe you are more talented than you think."

"Mm, I dunno," Zach mumbles.

"You can't be so shy and withdrawn, son. You gotta stand up for yourself, whoever you are. You know… thirteen years old! It's your time! You gotta start claiming who you are now, Zach," and he digs his spoon into his porridge. "You're going to be a great young man, I'm sure of it."

Zachary jumps up from his seat and goes over and hugs his dad.

"Ah, nice," Mr. Klossner says, dropping his spoon and fully giving into the embrace. Tristan looks on, feeling excluded. Mr. Klossner notices.

"And you are a super young woman," he says to her.

"Oh, so Zach's 'great' and I'm just 'super'?" she says.

"You are both Great and Super!"

"Kidding, Dad," she says. "But thanks."

Zachary lets go of him and returns to his seat and porridge.

"Listen, kids, I never planned to be doing this job. It sort of just happened. Your mom, she knew what she wanted, always did: to teach. And to teach something relevant, that would make people think," he says finally getting a mouthful of porridge in, swallowing, then continuing.

"I know you think that she's teaching University students and that can't relate to you and your lives, but it's not correct. Philosophy: Truth and Meaning, it's for everybody. Nothing is stronger than Truth, kids… "

"We know that, Dad," Tristan says.

"I know you know. But to LIVE it!"

"So, um, why then are you doing a job you don't really believe in?" she asks between porridge swallows.

"I told you, it happened that way. Your mother got her post at the university, a very important post, and we didn't want to be those kind of parents who both have jobs away from home and leave their children with paid nannies, or worse, nurseries where god-knows-who is raising your kid."

"So you mean… ?" Tristan holds her spoon still, getting the big picture.

"With my Masters in Film Studies, I took a job that I could do mostly at home, be with you when you were little, and then be around when you got home from school… "

"Dad… ," Tristan says dropping her spoon in her bowl. It clangs.

"'Dad', what? I did it gratefully, and I'd do it again. Okay, so sometimes I have to approve a film being made about a killer alligator or a man just out of prison trying to go straight but being led back into crime by his buddies… "

"Ending in extreme car chase… ," Tristan smiles.

"With fiery explosion at the end," Zach adds.

They all laugh.

"TRUTH, kids!"

"Jesus said 'The truth shall set you free'. And Walt Whitman said 'Whatever satisfies the soul is Truth'," Tristan remarks. "See? I do talk to Mom sometimes about her work."

"I'm impressed," her dad remarks.

"Dad… ," Zachary takes a gulp and puts his spoon in his bowl.

"Yes, son?"

"I… ," He hesitates. Tristan kicks him under table, and widens her eyes when he looks over to her.

"Well… something's going on… at school," he manages to let out.

"What do you mean, Zach?" he asks, sipping his tea. "A protest? Sports event? Rebuilding? Alien invasion? What?"

"No, I mean with… me. There's some other kids, bigger kids, that… you know… aren't nice to me."

"They're called Bullies, Zach. Let's use the word!" Tristan interjects.

"What, like bullying you badly?" his father asks.

"Is there good bullying… ?"

"No, of course not. What I meant was…I don't know what I meant."

"They pick on me… call me cruel names… and worse. In P.E. mostly, but also in classrooms, at lunch period… "

Tristan nudges him under the table again. Zachary continues.

"…. at the mall sometimes."

"Zach, this is serious. No kids can get away with bullying my son!"

"Um, Dad. Sounds like a line from one of those cheesy scripts," Tristan comments.

"Well, does your mother know? A teacher? Anybody?" his dad asks.

"Tris has seen it a bit… "

"At the mall. I defended him."

"And I told the nurse at school, and she's going to try to bring it up at a meeting or something. She's excused me from P.E. for awhile."

"Great, Zach," Tristan pats his shoulder.

"And yesterday I went to talk to Tante about it," Zachary adds.

"You didn't tell me that," Mr. Klossner says.

"You didn't tell me that," Tristan says too.

(Ah, but he did tell ME that! See? A dog IS Man's--or Young Kid's-- Best Friend. Numero Uno.)

"She was really kind," Zachary continues. "Oh, and I forgot: she gave me extra chocolate chip cookies to bring back, but, sorry, me and Leo ate them all up in the treehouse."

"What?" Tristan says.

"What?" Mr. Klossner says.

(What??? I say. Traitor!)

"Sorry, but we got hungry. Anyhow, Tante said that usually a bully's been bullied himself… or herself."

"Liberal Humanistic Rationale," Tristan remarks. Her father looks over at her.

"You really *have* been talking with your mother."

"Zach," she turns to her brother. "That might be true, but it's no excuse for people picking on other people."

"No, I know it's not. But it helps me to understand better that it is more about THEM then me. I mean, I never did ANYthing to this guy, so why's he bullying me?"

"'This guy'? There's one in particular?" his dad asks.

"There's one who does it the most, yeah."

"Is he the guy at the mall?" Tristan asks. Zachary nods.

"Creep," she adds.

"Yes, creep, but, Dad, did you know that Hitler first tried to be an artist and failed?" Zachary says.

"No, I didn't."

"He failed at Creating and turned to Destroying," Zachary says.

"Did Tante tell you that, too?" Tristan asks.

"Yeah, but… "

"Again, Zach. That is no rationale for his horrific behavior."

"Maybe not, but it makes more sense of it."

"Killing is killing, son."

"Yeah, but, like, we kill cows so we can eat hamburgers, and chickens when we go to KFC," Zachary exclaims.

"True," his father agrees.

"But they're animals, Zach. We're talking about the systematic genocide of people, BY people!" Tristan's voice rises.

"Yes, but he has a point, Tris. We also have Capital Punishment here in America. I mean, we say 'Killing is Wrong' and then we sanction killing people."

"I guess when you put it that way," Tristan agrees.

"But we're getting away from the issue here," Mr. Klossner says. "Zach, we need to do something about this bullying at school."

"Well, right now I have to brush my teeth and get ready or I miss my first class," Zachary says, getting up from the table.

As he passes, his dad puts out an arm and grabs Zachary and pulls him near, hugging him again.

"You're a brave boy, Zach. And I am SO proud of you!"

Then looking over at Tristan, alone again at the other end of the table.

"You, too Tris, defending him like that. I wish you kids had come to me earlier with this."

"We couldn't, Dad," Zachary says pulling away. "The elephant wasn't so clear until recently."

And he heads out and up the stairs.

"Elephant? I'm sorry, did I miss something here?" Mr. Klossner asks.

(You and me both, dude. I still say it's a pretty lame, obscure saying. Can't you humans just speak plainly and say 'Unaddressed Issue'? You always gotta drag us animals into it!

Which reminds me... this seems a good place to take a break from the heaviness of the topic and address another one. And it warrants its own chapter!)

CHAPTER 27½

Alright, listen up. I have finished compiling a list of sayings you humans use in which my beloved species is referred to, often with profound disrespect. Here it is:

ABUSE OF THE HONORABLE D-WORD
(Otherwise known as Verbal Bullying)

1) *'Gone to the dogs'—You say this for something or someone who's gone bad. Insulting to us dogs, pure and simple.*

2) *'It's raining cats and dogs'—None of us dogs understand what you could possibly be referring to when you use this. Worse, you list us second after cats!*

3) *'It's a dog eat dog world'—Excuse me, but when's the last time you saw a dog gobble up another dog? Hmm? Doesn't happen. EVER!*

4) *'Three dog night'—You say this when it is so cold that it would take three dogs to huddle up with to keep warm. Nice image, but you use it in a negative situation. Three dogs cuddled up can also be for Cuteness (see YouTube).*

5) '<u>Dog days of summer</u>'—*Then you do a complete about-face and use our species to mean Too Hot. Supposedly it's because in August a bright star you named The Dog Star rises and sets with the sun. But that's no excuse.*

6) '<u>Sick as a dog</u>'—*Not even worthy of a comment.*

7) '<u>Every dog has his day</u>'—*Meaning that everyone gets their revenge, eventually. Excuse me, but how do you connect the dots from Revenge-to-Dogs? Rather 'Every cat has his day', because we all know how vicious cats can be!*

8) '<u>Like a dog with two tails</u>'—*meaning So Happy that it's like a dog having two tails to show their happiness. Again, a misunderstanding, as we dogs wag our tails for feelings other than happiness--like when we feel guilty we wag it stiff and low. Any dog owner knows this simple fact.*

9) '<u>A hair of the dog that bit you</u>'—*Okay, this one is just WEIRD. It refers to drinking MORE alcohol to cure drinking TOO MUCH alcohol. Really! Apparently ancient Scottish people used to think you could cure a dog bite by rubbing it with a hair from the dog that bit you (a claim we totally dispute!). So 'like with like': drank too much? The cure is to have one more! I really worry about your species.*

10) '<u>A dog by any other name would smell as sweet</u>'—*I realize that you assume this saying*

actually refers to roses, but I have been informed by older and wiser dogs at the Shelter where it's been passed down for generations, that, in fact, the British writer Shakespeare originally referred to us dogs in his initial manuscript, then later changed it to roses at the insistence of his cat Macbeth.
True Story!

I hope this list causes you to reconsider using our name in vain. If it makes it any easier, simply replace the word 'dog' in each saying with the word 'cat'. It would be more appropriate.

And if you don't know that word, look it up!

CHAPTER 28

During History class the next day, a note is delivered to class by an older student, and Mr. Foley walks over and hands it to Zachary. Hesitantly he opens it.

It is hand-written on paper with a letterhead of the school principal and reads:

Zachary B. Klossner,

Please report to Nurse Wells' office after your lunch break today.

Sincerely,

Patric Meredith

Principal

A shiver runs up his spine. And then back down again.

'This is it', he thinks to himself. 'No backing out now. The elephant's about to be dragged into public.'

He finds Leo waiting at their special hiding place at lunch break, and pulls out his peanut butter and honey sandwich, unwraps it and takes a bite. Leo's already eaten half of his cheese sandwich.

"Camembert, from France," he says, then takes another bite.

"Pretty good," he adds, smiling. "But last night for dinner she made Cauliflower Cheese with something from France that smelled like moldy rags. Awful!"

"I got a note to report to Mrs. Wells after lunch," Zachary suddenly blurts out.

"Oh… " Leo responds. "Oh… so… it's happening."

"I don't know. It doesn't give details, just to go see her."

"Oh… "

"What, 'oh'?"

Leo puts his sandwich down in his lap. A pigeon overhead on a branch is eyeing it.

"Well, I mean… I'm a little worried that if Padilla or any of the other guys find out, it could get worse."

"Yeah, if my name's involved," Zachary says.

"Yeah, right. And then I'm your best friend, so I'd be next in line for revenge."

"She promised me it'd be confident."

"Confident? Who's confident here?"

"No, she says it also means 'kept secret'… Oh, wait, no. It's 'confidential'. That's it."

"Whatever you call it, I certainly hope so, dude, or you and me are goners," he says picking up his sandwich again. The pigeon flies off.

"You know, like in the old movies the mafia guys put heavy weights on peoples' legs and drop them in the sea!" Leo adds.

"I hope not. I don't swim so well," Zachary says biting into his sandwich.

"Dude, with fifty pounds of iron tied to your foot, swimming doesn't matter,' Leo explains. "You sink! Like, fast!"

"Oh… "

"Yeah, oh… "

They finish their sandwiches, Zachary then takes out an apple and Leo a banana and two huge molasses cookies that his mom made, one of which he offers to Zachary.

"In case it's our last cookie on earth."

When the 12:50 bell rings, Leo rushes off to his English class, and Zachary takes the long hidden way behind buildings and small corridors that he has memorized by now, to arrive to the Administration building. He walks down the wood-panel corridor to the end and knocks.

Nobody replies, and he tries the knob but it is locked.

'Great,' he thinks with relief. 'No one here, so I can still back out and leave.'

As he turns around to go, Mrs. Wells appears coming out of the Principal's office, sees him, and rushes towards him.

"Sorry, Zachary," she says almost out of breath.

"It's Zach… "

"Zach, yes, sorry. Emergency meeting with Mr. Meredith. Seems some parents are making their voices louder about their kids having to say the Pledge of Allegiance," she says nearly panting, unlocking her door, and gesturing him in first. She suddenly realizes that she has said too much, that she shouldn't be revealing official details like that to a young student, but it is too late.

"Why don't they like it?" Zachary asks, though he finds it rather lame himself, and doesn't even understand half the words he has to say, hand over heart, every day in first period. He takes off his backpack and sits on the patient bed.

"Well, you know, the 'one nation under God' bit. Oh, and off the bed. Come sit here. You're not a patient today."

Zachary gets up and sits in the chair near Mrs. Wells.

"My mom says it's hypo… hippo… "

"Hypocritical? " she suggests, sitting down in her chair.

"Yeah that, because something about, um…"

"Separation of Church and State."

"Yeah, that."

"Well, your mom's right. This country was founded on the principal's of Freedom of Speech, Freedom of Religion, so why are Muslim or Jewish or atheist kids forced to pledge to a Christian god? "

"And I don't understand it all, like the word 'indivisible'."

"It means 'not separable', Zach, that the States are united. Anyhow, to discuss the Constitution is not why we're here today, as I'm sure you can guess. Although, Bullyism, if that's a word, is also disconnected from the American Ideal which promises Life, Liberty and the Pursuit of Happiness to every citizen, of which you are one," she says spinning around in her chair to face Zachary.

"A bully is denying you your liberties as well as your happiness," she adds.

"That's for sure!"

"So, listen, I brought up Bullying at the meeting last Friday, and principal Meredith was fully sympathetic, and wants to pursue the issue. In fact, between you and me, he was bullied a bit himself and understands how debilitating it can be."

"Debil… "

"Sorry. How draining it can be on your energy," she explains.

"And on your pocket money!" Zachary adds.

"How so?"

"Some older kids force the seventh graders to give them money if they don't wanna get beat up. You see it all the time in the cafeteria."

"That's extortion!"

"Huh?"

"Extortion. It's when you demand money by force or threats."

"It's just mean!"

"That, too. Anyhow, Principal Meredith wants to meet with you. I'll take you over shortly to his office."

"I've never been sent to the principal before… "

"You're not being sent, Zach. It's… well, it's being invited."

"Will you be there, too?"

"If you'd feel better, yes, I can stay, too."

"I would. I mean, I don't know Mr. Meredith… "

"He's a nice man, Zach. Don't worry. So… ready? He's expecting you."

Zachary stands up and flings his backpack on, and the two walk out of her office, down the hallway, and past the numerous large framed photos of past graduating classes. Zachary looks at them as they pass, sometimes catching a particular date—1997, 1982, 1976, 1964, 1955—or a face, eyes looking out at him.

"I wonder how many of them were bullied?" he says.

"Oh, a lot I imagine," Mrs. Wells comments, "but things were hushed-up more back then." She knocks at the door marked 'PRINCIPAL—Patric Meredith'.

"Come in," a voice says on the other side of the door, and she opens it and leads Zachary in.

Mr. Meredith sits at a desk much bigger than Mrs. Wells', but the room is much smaller than her office, and Zachary figures that's because she needs a bed and all those cabinets for different medicines and stuff.

'But there are no pills to stop you being bullied', he says to himself as Mr. Meredith rises from his chair and crosses over to greet him.

He's a pleasant looking man, a little short and stocky, and slightly balding, but with a kid's face and deep dark eyes that seem to smile themselves.

"Zachary Klossner, I'm very glad to finally meet you. I've heard so much about you. All from Mrs. Wells, of course," he says as he shakes Zachary's hand softly.

"Thanks," Zachary says shyly, sitting down in one of the two dark wood chairs in front of the desk.

"Zach would feel better if I stayed," Mrs. Wells informs him.

"Yes, of course, Judith," the principal says, gesturing for her to take the other seat.

'Judith', Zachary says to himself. 'So that's her name. Judith, Judy, Jude…'

While the principal looks down at a paper, Zachary notices an American flag and a smaller one for California with a grizzly bear on it behind the principal's desk to one side, and leans into Mrs. Wells whispering.

"I'll bet HE doesn't say the Pledge of Allegiance to God every morning."

"No, I'll bet he doesn't. As an adult you get to make more choices than as a kid," she whispers back. "Anyways… ," she says more quietly, "he's Buddhist," and winks an eye. Zachary smiles.

"Zachary, Mrs. Wells has informed me of the situation you've been experiencing here at Jarvis Middle School, and let me be the first to apologize, and then assure you that no bullying of any kind will be tolerated. So, I'm deeply concerned, not only for your welfare, of course, but that you imply Mr. Parnell seems to witness, even encourage it."

"Yes, sir," Zachary replies quietly.

"Would you tell me, please, *how* he encourages it, because this is deeply worrying. A teacher's job, besides the imparting of knowledge to his or her pupils, is to see that they are well and safe under their care. So, tell me."

"Well… the worst thing is that he always picks the tough kids to be the team captains knowing they'll pick all their friends to be on their team, and then just stop when there are three or four weaker kids, and he just throws us on a team while the captains groan and complain and Mr. Parnell just smiles."

"Well, Mr. Parnell should explain to the captains, to all of you, in fact, that sports is about team spirit and fair play. YOU should be picked as captain sometimes."

"Yeah, right. THAT would never happen. And, besides that, the tough guys do their bullying often right in front of Mr. Parnell and he doesn't lift a finger to stop it. But that happens in many classrooms with many teachers. It's not just him."

"Well, this is intolerable."

"Mrs. Wells used that word, too," Zachary remarks.

"It means unacceptable, wrong. And I'm truly sorry that it's been happening right here under my leadership. I promise you, Zachary, that it will be addressed at once. Mrs. Wells and I and Vice Principal Spencer worked all weekend on an appendage to The Standards of Practice and Leadership which has been put in all the teachers' boxes this morning, and at this Friday's staff meeting we shall be discussing this one subject only."

"Good. I hope," Zachary says.

"Not hope, Zachary. I promise you that every teacher will be required to address any bullying they witness in their class at once with the offending students. And if it persists, the students' parents will be notified. And if we see no changes, and the bullying continues, we shall call a Parent-Teacher meeting which I will also attend, and we'll figure out how to approach the problem. Really, I was mortified…"

"Shocked," Mrs. Wells leans into Zachary, explaining the word.

"… to hear that you and other kids have had to endure this at my school, Zachary. My deepest apologies."

"And you won't use my name in this? I mean, nobody knows it's me who snitched?" Zachary asks.

"It's not snitching when you let others know that some horrible thing is occurring. Especially one that's, quite frankly, illegal. If this was happening between adults, the courts would put a restraining order on the offender."

"We're not to be naïve here either, Mr. Meredith," Mrs. Wells suddenly interjects. "Some mild forms of bullying, like calling each other names, or making fun of their hairdo or outfits, always takes place, and will continue to. Kids at this age are trying to discover who they are and what they want to become, with some fighting to be heard, to dominate others…"

"I get that. Mrs. Wells and I are sympathetic to the raging hormones and fight-for-identity and all that stuff that young teenagers are going through. Nonetheless, on this I'm quite fervent.... "

"Strong-willed," she explains to Zachary.

"... No Bullying will be tolerated while I'm in charge here. I knew it existed, yes, of course, mildly. But what Zachary's telling us here is a systematic status quo to perpetrate and encourage a bullying atmosphere which I find reprehensible... "

"Disgusting,"

"... and downright vile."

"Also disgusting."

"So I hope we are all on the same page here," Mr. Parnell concludes.

"Absolutely!" Mrs. Wells nods.

"Yeah, sure. Please!" Zachary nods.

"Fine," Mr. Meredith rises from his chair. "Let's see how the teachers respond to the morning's memo, and I look forward to reinforcing it at Friday's meeting. Mrs. Wells, Zachary, I thank you both for your input."

There is a pause as Mr. Meredith stands looking over at them seated.

Mrs. Wells rises and nudges Zachary to do so, and they quietly leave his office.

Outside in the hallway Mrs. Wells turns to Zachary.

"So, well, that's it for now. As he said, 'Let's see how it goes'. Thank you, Zachary... Zach. I'm going to miss you coming into my office during your P.E. classes."

"But I don't have to go back to P.E. now, do I?" he asks, worried.

"No, dear, you're still exempt for the time being. You can volunteer in the Faculty Office during those periods, and maybe we'll pass in the hallway. Meanwhile, we want the dust to settle and the storm to pass."

(Again! 'The dust to settle and the storm to pass'? What dust? What storm? And by the way, that's a pretty silly mixing of two unrelated metaphors.

We dogs are more straight-forward. If a big Saint Bernard was picking on a dachshund, we'd bark at the bigger one and say in dog language, 'Hey, tough guy! Haven't you got better things to do? Why pick on that little guy? It's an unfair match. Go pee on a tree trunk or chase a ball or something if you need a distraction. But leave the dachshund dude alone!'

If that doesn't work we show our teeth and snarl. And if THAT doesn't work, we attack!

But just enough to send the tough guy whimpering away, tail between the legs, lesson learned. One hopes.)

CHAPTER 29

The week passes smoothly at school for Zachary. Not having to attend P.E. classes reduces the chances of him being bullied by 60%. But he still moves carefully and cautiously through the corridors and in and out of classes in case of the other 40%.

Leo tells him that he's been cutting P.E. all week when they meet on Friday for their hidden lunch break.

"Maybe you're getting Anthropophobia," Zachary says.

"What's that?"

"Fear of People."

"It's not a fear of people, but of *certain* people," Leo says. Then, "Hey, is there a name for Fear of Bullies?"

"Hmm. Don't know. I'll look it up. But there *is* one called Tris-kai-dek-a-phobia."

"What the bleep is that?"

"Fear of being thirteen."

"Oh god, I hope there's not one of those for every age from now until death. Otherwise, what's the point?" Leo reaches into his lunch bag for his sandwich.

"Which reminds me. Death and Heath and Health," Leo suddenly blurts out.

"What? Death and… what?"

"Death and Heath and Health. Spelled the same but pronounced differently. "

"Oh… ," Zachary responds. "Where do you come up with these?"

"With what?" Leo asks.

"All these weird English thingies."

"When I wake up in the middle of the night, ya know, and just lie there, they come to me."

"Huh, not me. When I can't sleep I'm always thinking about how I can avoid being picked on the next day at school!"

Then they talk about the meeting that's going to take place after school between the principal and teachers to discuss bullying.

"Do you think anything will change after the meeting?" Leo asks through a mouthful of cheese sandwich. Then smiling, "Oh, cheddar again! Yes!" but not noticing the pigeon on the branch above him, head bobbing, watching for any crumbs to drop for a later retrieval.

"I don't know if things will change," Zachary answers him. "I hope so. It depends on the teachers, really. If they're concerned and care enough to do something about it."

"Well, I mean, why would they not care?" Leo asks between bites.

"They've let it go on this long right in front of their eyes!" Zachary says before biting into his peanut butter with honey sandwich. "It's like there's an elephant in every classroom!" he says with his mouth full.

"So, um... let me get this straight. The idea is we all gotta look at the elephant and... what?" Leo asks and then takes a huge bite, a large hunk of bread falling to the ground and duly noted by overhead pigeon.

"Well, we all gotta look at it first, instead of pretending it's not there. I guess that's what's today's meeting is: finally looking at the elephant."

"Hmm. Hey, maybe if they served the coffee and donuts at the meeting with, like, napkins with elephant pictures on them it would be more obvious," Leo suggests.

Zachary considers replying but rolls his eyes instead.

On the last bite of Leo's sandwich he makes a twisted face and pulls a small bit of chewed-up sandwich out of his mouth.

"Ooh, cat hair. Or mom hair. Ick!" and spits the rest out onto the ground below.

And the pigeon waits anxiously for them to leave.

The meeting after school that day takes place in the Faulty Lounge with no elephant napkins. A couple of teachers do not show up and Mr. Meredith takes note of their names.

"I said 'Mandatory' and I meant it, folks. No fooling around on this issue. I want it resolved and I mean starting Monday first class of the day!" he says.

All of the teachers are now aware of how serious their principal is taking this, and they shift in their seats and prepare to be fully attentive and compliant.

('Compliant', adjective: to agree with others or with rules and regulations.

See, I can take over for Mrs. Wells any old day: I know lots of big words, I can assist in human problems with my charm and a dewy-eyed dog-look, and I can heal all manner of wounds with a good lick.

And don't go 'Eww!' Look it up: dog saliva is cleaner than human saliva, so there!

I'd only have difficulty if there was lots of blood and guts involved. Then I get rather squeamish! Like Zach!)

CHAPTER 30

"Okay listen, I thought of another one," Leo tells Zachary as they munch on granola bars up in the treehouse on Saturday afternoon. They've hoisted Gwendolyn up in the basket, and she cowers now in the corner, afraid of heights.

(Okay, so I share that in common with that dippy little poodle, BUT THAT'S ALL!)

Leo grabs a notebook and pen they keep stashed under a loose board in the wall which is full of secret plans, new ways to blow up stuffed animals, the vomit recipe, and the bad cuss words they keep hearing from the older kids at school but don't know quite what they all mean.

"I USE this pen," Leo writes on a blank page. "Sounds like 'yooz', right? Now look— 'The pen's USE is to write'. Sounds like 'yoos'. Same word and same spelling, slightly different meaning and way different sound."

"Oh, yeah, true," Zachary says half-heartedly. "You're right, I guess. English is crazy."

"Hey, what's the matter, Zach? You're like all jittery and stuff. That's your favorite granola bar and you've barely bit off any yet."

Zachary puts the granola bar down and shifts his position on the wood-slat floor.

"Mrs. Wells called my parents last night. She wants them to come into speak with her and the principal today at four o'clock."

"Oh. You don't think they're blaming you for this… ?"

"What do you mean?"

"Well, why would they want to meet your parents? It's happening to *you*, not them!"

"No, sorry… I'm supposed to go in too."

"Oh… "

"Yeah, 'oh'."

"But, hey, that's a good thing, no? It must mean they're really taking it all seriously," Leo says.

"Yeah, I guess. But I'm a little worried. I mean, when it was just happening to me, okay, it wasn't nice, but I could try to handle it. But now, me telling and everybody getting involved… I don't know what's gonna happen. They're taking it over. I mean, well, what if they make it worse? What if Padilla finds out it was me who squealed on him?"

"But you like Mrs. Wells and the principal, right?"

"Well, yeah."

"And you trust them?"

"I guess so… yeah."

"Then maybe we just have to leave it to the grown-ups to deal with. I mean, the grownups who are most responsible are Mr. and Mrs. Padilla, raising a psycho son!"

"Leo, there is no Mrs. Padilla," Zachary says trying to chew on some granola bar, but feeling nauseous when it goes down.

"What do you mean? He was born without a mother? Is that possible?"

"No, he *had* a mother, but she died when he was three or something. Mrs. Wells found out and told me yesterday when I went to volunteer at the Faculty Office."

"Oh, bummer, just a dad, huh?"

"And not a very nice one, she said. He drinks too much beer and stuff like your Uncle Dario, and acts all odd and doesn't take care of the kids."

"Kids? Joe's got, like, brothers and sisters?"

"Yeah. There's four children and Joe's the youngest, and the other kids are all boys, and they, like, pick on him and stuff."

"How does Mrs. Wells know all this?" Leo asks finishing his granola bar. Zachary then hands him his and Leo starts in on it.

"She said after I came in and told her everything, you know, and gave her Joe's name, she called him into her office, saying a lie, that she noticed a big bruise on his arm and was worried about it."

"But there IS a big bruise, she's right."

"Yeah, I know. We never thought about why he has that bruise all the time. She found out."

"You mean, like, BHAM!" Leo punches his fist into the air.

"Yep. Padilla gets bullied at home by his father and brothers."

"Wow… I feel sorta sad for him now."

"I know. Me too."

"Well… I mean… maybe just her talking to him, and he telling about his problems at home, maybe that'll make him think about bullying *us* and how bad *that* feels, too."

"You mean, maybe him confronting the elephant in his own living room will make it better for all of us?"

"Maybe. I hope so."

"I'm more confused now than before… , " Zachary says zipping up his hoodie and getting ready to get up.

"Yeah, that throws a spanner in the works."

"Huh?"

"My dad says it. It's British. Spanner means wrench."

"I still don't get it."

"'Throw a wrench in the works'. To ruin things. They say 'boot' over there for car trunk, too."

"Huh… ?"

"In England. I saw it last night in a British film. 'Put yer bags in the boot, there lad', some taxi driver said."

"Okay, whatever. I gotta go," Zachary says standing up. "Mom made a quiche for lunch and then we all go to the principal's office together."

"Wait. Your mom made a kiss?"

"No, a quiche. It's some French eggy-cheesy thing. She says she made it before when I was like five, but I don't remember."

Zachary starts climbing down from the tree-house, knowing that each step he now takes, the descent to the ground, then the walk home, and later to the principal's office, will change his whole life.

Maybe.

Hopefully.

(Quiche, Kiss, Koss, Kish! Who cares what it's called if it's CHEESY?!

And thinking about that Joe dude not having a mother reminds me-- I forgot to include in my story that the Heffernans had me fixed, so I cannot be a mother and have a bunch of furry little Cassia Juniors.

Speaking of Crazy English: why do you call it 'getting fixed' when, excuse me, nothing was broken??)

CHAPTER 31

Mr. Klossner parks his Karmann Ghia in the faculty parking lot at Jarvis Middle School later that afternoon as the Principal had directed him to. No teachers on Saturdays, so the faculty spaces are all free, he told Mr. Klossner on the phone when they set up the meeting.

They took the Karmann Ghia and not his mother's Toyota because Zachary requested it. Dad's car is a lot more fun, like a cartoon car, and Zachary said they'd need all the fun they could squeeze out of the afternoon, since most of it, he was certain, would not be.

Mr. Klossner even let Zachary sit up front while he drove so he wouldn't get car sick, Mrs. Klossner in the back. They had stopped at the gelato place after a lunch at home of quiche and salad, and Zachary just stuck to plain vanilla—he wasn't in the mood to try a new gelato flavor in the midst of the day's drama.

Mr. Klossner ordered Pistachio Paradise.

Mrs. Klossner declined (though she took a quick lick of the pistachio out of curiosity).

"My weight! No more gelato or cookies until I lose ten pounds!" she said while staring at all the gelato flavors and colors in the freezer display case.

"Okay, just a sample spoon of the Fabulous Fig," she finally gave in. But that was all (that and the lick of her husband's cone).

They walked back to the car in the mall parking lot while the father and son licked at their cones. Nobody spoke. They all knew where they were off to next, and why, and it just seemed too big to put into a few words in a parking lot licking ice cream cones.

"Zach," Mrs. Klossner finally looked over at him and spoke. "I… I just want to say… well, two things. One: I am SO proud of you, son, for facing up to this. And, two: that I'm sorry we didn't see it ourselves, or were too busy or distracted or whatever… I feel awful that you've been going through this on your own."

'Okay, Mom's not only staring at the elephant, but she's jumped up on its back and is riding it!' Zachary thought to himself.

She reached over and put her arm around his shoulder, rubbing his back.

Nothing more was said. Silence, as they finished their gelato leaning on dad's car in the large parking lot of the mall.

Zachary's mom kept rubbing his back. And he didn't squirm away. He let her. And it comforted him.

And now they are sitting in the car for a lingering moment after Mr. Klossner shuts off the engine in the faculty parking lot at Zachary's school.

"Well… ," he says unbuckling his seat belt and opening his door to get out.

Zachary and his mom follow, and Zachary leads them to the Administrative building and down the wood-paneled hallway to the door marked PRINCIPAL. Mr. Klossner lightly knocks, and the door swings open on its own.

Inside, the principal sits behind his desk with Mrs. Wells in a chair alongside him. In front of the desk in a semi circle are five chairs, the two dark wood ones usually there, and three others brought in from the Faculty Lounge. Mr. Meredith rises and shakes the hands of Zachary's parents and pats Zachary sweetly on the head, and then they are introduced to Mrs. Wells.

"She's the one I told you about," Zachary whispers to his parents as they all sit down into three of the five chairs. Zachary is curious why there are two empty seats as well, but the second he begins to ponder it, Mr. Meredith starts to talk.

"Let me thank you first for coming in on such short notice, but we thought we should really address this issue immediately for the sake of all concerned. Zachary was brave enough, or desperate enough, to confide in Mrs. Wells about an intolerable situation here at Jarvis Middle School. There's only one appropriate word for it—Bullying. Older, bigger, tougher students picking on younger, weaker ones, sometimes rather aggressively. Mrs. Wells then wisely came to me with his secret, and not only did we devise a plan to confront the main perpetrator…"

"Wait, the what?" Zachary interrupts. "Sorry, I don't know that word."

"That's okay, Zachary. I want you to understand everything that goes on in here today. A perpetrator is, well… "

Mrs. Wells jumps in.

"It's somebody who commits a crime," she explains.

"Okay, got it."

"Right. So… where was I?" Mr. Meredith asks.

Now it's Zachary's turn to jump in.

"'A plan to confront the mean per-pe-trater'."

"Main, not mean, Zachary… "

"Main AND mean," he says.

"Well, yes, okay, true. Anyhow, Mrs. Wells called in the boy under a pretext and carefully got his own story out of him. She didn't have to mention any bullying, but just the large bruise on his arm, showing concern, and he started telling about his hard life at home."

"It just poured out, like he needed to confront it," Mrs. Wells adds.

"I guess you can't ignore an elephant in the room for too long before you just *gotta* look at it," Zachary comments. "I mean, an elephant is HUGE!"

"Yes, that's right, Zach," Mr. Klossner says, smiling proudly at his son.

"So I and Mrs. Wells feel the best way to deal with this is to confront head-on all the participants at once," and he turns to Mrs. Wells and nods. She gets up and leaves the room.

Then he turns to Zachary and looks at him directly.

"Zachary, I've asked Joe Padilla and his father to join us. They're waiting in the Faculty Lounge and Mrs. Wells will bring them in shortly… "

He stops when he notices Zachary tense up nervously.

"Nothing bad is going to happen, nor *will* happen, in consequence of what takes place, I promise you that. The best way to deal with a horrific secret is to just bring it out into the open fast and furiously."

'Fast and Furious'. Bad movie,' Zachary comments to himself. 'All seven of them!' And then realizes that if he can think of movies right now, and make a joke, the situation can't be all that horrible anymore.

He takes a deep breath, the kind Tristan has been showing him to get relaxed, and prepares to look Joe Padilla, his bully, in the eyes.

(Um, excuse me… I hope I'm not interrupting anything crucial here, but I just finished an appendage to my list, and feel it might be appropriate to the current situation:

ABUSE OF THE HONORABLE D-WORD
(Appendage)

10) '*It's a dog's life*'—which you say to mean that life has been hard and unpleasant. *(like Joe Padilla's at home)*

11) '*A barking dog never bites*'—used when somebody makes threats but does not necessarily carry them through. *(also Joe Padilla....so far)*

12) '*You can't teach an old dog a new trick*'--that it is difficult to make somebody change the way they do something when they've been doing it a long time. *(you better hope this one is NOT about Joe Padilla)*

13) '*I've got to see a man about a dog*'—this just means you gotta go to the bathroom. *Which refers to Zachary at this very moment, because he just left the Principal's office to go take a pee.)*

CHAPTER 32

Zachary returns from the restroom, sits back down and takes another deep breath, knowing that at any moment he is going to come face to face with his bully, Joe Padilla.

Only that doesn't quite happen.

When Mrs. Wells finally escorts them in, Joe and Mr. Padilla take the empty seats and Joe appears just as timid and scared as Zachary imagines he must look when Joe is bullying him—he looks down at his shoes, making no contact with anybody.

"Mr. Padilla, Joe, you both know why we are all here," Mr. Meredith speaks. "I've explained the situation to you over the phone, as much as we know. This is Zachary Klossner who Joe has been bullying, among others, for some time now."

Neither Mr. Padilla nor Joe speak a word, nor make any gesture.

"We are not here to criminalize, for that just increases the cycle of abuse, but we ARE here to face this issue head-on, here and now. Now I know there are many kids who bully, that Joe is not alone in this, but we are here to resolve this particular dynamic. The larger issue of Bullying, Mrs. Wells, myself, and the Vice principal will address with new procedures for the teachers, and with an open-door policy for the students to report any abuse they are facing, however small. It is Zero-Tolerance to Bullying from now on. And I mean ZERO."

Zachary has to pee again—too much water after the gelato—but doesn't dare move.

Mrs. Wells jumps in.

"Part of the new procedures, Mr. Padilla, is to try and bring in the parents of the kids involved. Bullying is a personal issue regarding individuals, and we will deal with it that way. Do you understand, sir?" she asks Mr. Padilla. He is silent and barely raises his head.

(14) 'Beware of a silent dog and still water'—A saying in Ancient Rome to mean that both could be hiding dangers. Sorry, I just got to get that one in.)

"Mr. Padilla....?" she asks again.

"Yes I do, ma'am," Mr. Padilla finally replies.

"Good. Because we understand there is some trouble at home for Joe as well, and though it is a personal matter of the family, if we discover there are any criminal acts occurring, any form of Domestic Violence, it's our duty to report it through legal channels. Do you understand what I am saying, sir?"

"I do," he says again.

"We will be keeping a watch and interviewing Joe on a regular basis," Mr. Meredith says. "And if you need any assistance in this matter, Mr. Padilla, I can help steer you in the right direction for obtaining the proper help via counseling or State Assistance. But, that's another issue. Right now I'm deeply concerned with what takes place on our campus, in our classrooms…"

"And sports fields," Mrs. Wells interjects.

"And locker rooms," Zachary adds.

"… Exactly. Joe's behavior has been unacceptable, though we sympathize with his own personal issue… "

(Because his father is:

15) 'Meaner than a junkyard dog'—which you say to mean 'cruel', though personally I've met some junkyard dogs that are the sweet sensitive type.)

"… and again, I and Mrs. Wells are here for you, Joe, we want you to know that. ANYtime. Okay?"

Mr. Meredith looks directly over at Joe, who nods slightly without looking up.

"Bullying in any form... Let me repeat: BULLYING IN ANY FORM will not be tolerated here at Jarvis Middle School... not any longer. Oh, I know kids call each other names, sometimes cruel ones, and judge each other by their hair and fashions and stuff--that's the unfortunate status quo of teenagers in this day and age and culture. But that's not what truly concerns us. What does concern us is the systematic and aggressive taunting... "

'There's that word again', Zachary says to himself. 'I wonder if Tante was ever taunted?'

"... pushing, or mistreating which in any manner dehumanizes of students by other students. Do I make myself crystal clear?"

They all nod.

"Joe, Zachary, I want you two to get up, cross over, and shake hands," Mr. Meredith says standing up behind his desk.

Zachary hesitates until his dad nudges him.

Joe rises, keeping his glance to the floor.

(He has what you humans would call:

16) *'A hang dog expression'—meaning one of self pity and shame.)*

"Won't do, Joe," Mr. Meredith adds. "Besides shaking his hand, you need to look him in the eye. This is another human being you've been mistreating. A boy, like yourself, trying to discover who he is. So, head up, look Zachary in the eyes, and I want you to shake his hand and apologize to him."

Joe looks up quickly, shakes his hand and mumbles "Sorry."

"I'm sorry, too," Zachary then says out loud, surprising Joe and causing him to look up into Zachary's eyes.

"I know it's not all your fault," Zachary adds. And he thinks he spots a bit of water forming in Joe's eyes.

"Good one, boys," Mr. Meredith says. "Back to your seats. Now, I'm not dumb. I know you can't resolve such an endemic problem in one weekend meeting… "

"What's a demic?" Zachary scrunches his face.

"It means Prevalent, um… common," Mrs. Wells says.

Mr. Meredith nods and continues.

"So Mrs. Wells will be checking up with Zachary and Joe weekly, and they are both required to attend these private meetings with her. Is that clear?"

Zachary nods. Joe does not.

"Joe, I mean it. The Bullying stops RIGHT NOW. The eyes of all my staff will be on every one of you kids from now on, and they will be taking Bathroom Watch at each break as well. On Monday we'll have a rally after lunch in which I will address the entire student body in the gym on this very issue."

He pauses for a moment.

"Look, I'm not innocent in all this," he says solemnly. "If this has transpired under my guidance, I am as guilty as anybody, and I take partial blame for your suffering, Zachary. And yours, Joe. I apologize to you both and ask your forgiveness. But what's done is done, and now is now. And from this moment on, I will make the issue of Bullying a top priority for myself and every one of my staff."

He looks over to Mrs. Wells.

"Anything to add?"

"No, I think you said it all," Mrs. Wells says. But then adds "Just to remind you, boys, I am here anytime you need to talk, about this or any other issue—always in confidence and always assured that I will follow any thing through to the best of my ability. Promise."

"So, now, no more elephants in my classrooms," Mr. Meredith concludes. "And I thank you all for coming. Mr. Padilla, will you stay on a moment, please?"

They all rise. Mr. and Mrs. Klossner both pat their son Zachary and tell him how proud they are of him.

As they turn to leave, Zachary notices that Mr. Padilla doesn't look at Joe at all, or say anything to him. Zachary takes a deep breath and moves away from his parents and walks over towards the two Padilla men.

He passes Joe, and puts his hand on Mr. Padilla's shoulder, looking him straight in the eyes.

"I wanna thank you for coming, sir," he says.

Mr. Padilla hesitates, his eyes seem to water as this young innocent kid stands before him showing respect and gratitude. Slowly he puts out his hand, and Zachary puts out his, and they meet mid-air, grab and shake.

Mr. Padilla then drops his head down same as his son's, and Zachary thinks he sees water forming in his eyes, too.

Zachary rejoins his parents at the door, and they slowly walk down the wood-paneled hall-way, hundreds of faces of old students staring out at them as they pass. Zachary looks up at them and wonders what became of them all.

Where they are now. How they each survived school and went on and did things, important things maybe, with their lives.

And then he wonders what HE will be doing with his life when some other 13-year-old passes through this hallway in later years and looks up and sees a photo with Zachary's face looking down at him? Will he have moved on from this drama, and passed through many more, and have found a place of contentment and fulfillment with his life?

Then he and his parents hit open the double doors at the end of the hallway, sunlight pouring in.

"Well, that went pretty well, I thought," Mr. Klossner comments as they head for the Faculty Parking lot.

"Yes," Mrs. Klossner agrees, tears forming in her eyes now, too.

"Yeah, and even Principal Meredith knew about elephants being in the classrooms. Did you hear him?"

"Yes, we heard him, Zach," his mother says putting her arm over his shoulder.

"How come I've been alive thirteen years and never knew before that there could be an elephant standing in the middle of the room with nobody noticing? Are there going to be more when I get older?"

"Probably, son, yes. There are lots of elephants in lots of rooms," Mr. Klossner says putting his arm over Zachary's other shoulder.

"If there's so many, why don't people just… SEE them?"

"Good question," Mr. Klossner says. "I don't know the answer to that."

"What do YOU think, Zach?" his mom asks.

"I think maybe some people really aren't even aware they're there," Zachary says, then laughs.

"What's that for?" his mother asks as they arrive to dad's little orange car.

"I just said 'they're there'. Leo keeps telling me about crazy things in the English language, like there are three 'theres': 'over *there*', '*their* car', and *they're* like 'they are'."

"Hmm. True," his mom says.

"So… you can actually say, um… 'they're over there by their car'."

"Yeah, that *is* pretty crazy," his dad smirks as he opens the car door.

Zachary opens the passenger door and slips in the front seat, his mom again in the back.

"Yeah, but that's not as crazy as 'they're over there by their elephant' and nobody even notices it!" Zachary adds as his dad starts the engine and they drive off for home.

Then change their minds and turn towards the outdoor mall and more gelato.

Zachary decides to be brave and try a totally new flavor, going for the most weird one— bright orange Marvelous Mango.

His dad sticks with Dangerously Dark Chocolate, and his mom still refuses, though she does try three sample spoons.

(And do they order any take-away for their beloved dog? No!

I'll just have to wait here on the couch until they get home for some cuddles.

Cuddles are way better than gelato anyway, if truth be told.)

CASSANDRA'S EPILOGUE

Nice happy gelato-gooey ending, right?

Well, not exactly. Almost nobody changes overnight after years of habit. Even I took a long time, you may recall, to get used to not being called Bobolina or Beckett or Jasmine or Cuddles, and to settle on Cassandra, the Greek princess (and prophet!)

So it took Joe some time to realize that bullying other classmates was maybe not the best way to deal with his frustrations at home. His dad tried to be a little kinder to him, but he had his own habit—he drank to forget that his wife died and he was now the sole parent to four sons. Four! Sons!!

Losing his wife was sort of like an elephant in his heart, I guess.

So maybe that's how all this bullying starts, same like with my first family, the Heffernans. They didn't mean to be bullies, but Mr. Heffernan had some bad feelings inside, did not look fully at them, and took it out on me (Imagine! Cute Moi!)

Anyway, over the following weeks, then months, Mrs. Wells had to call Joe into private meetings, some alone, some with Zachary present, and slowly, slowly, over time things calmed down for them both.

Leo noticed it as well, and eventually there came a day—it wasn't until late Spring—that he and Zachary could actually have their lunch out in the open quad in the sunlight, Zachary with his peanut butter and honey sandwich on whole wheat bread and Leo with some foreign cheese called 'Gouda'.

"Boring!" is all Leo said before throwing the other half in the trashcan, pissing off a pigeon or two. Zachary offered him half of his sandwich, which Leo was thankful for.

So they stayed good friends, sort of Comrades Against Adversity (and if you don't know what that word means, Google it, because Mrs. Wells isn't here to explain it to you.)

Zach would often come home from school and call me into his room to tell me how things were progressing at school—how the new Zero-Tolerance for Bullying was actually having some affect, and how if the teachers witnessed any students taunting (yes, that word again!) other kids, they would have them stay after class to tell them in private that such behavior isn't nice, and 'How would you like it if somebody called YOU 'four eyes' or 'drama freak' or 'nerd' or 'queer' or 'jew boy' or 'rag head' or 'beastie' or 'psycho' or 'tubby'? Or any of the other charming terms you humans come up with to try and degrade others.

Sometimes talking to the bullies worked immediately and sometimes it didn't. Some kids are pretty tough cookies… oops, there I go again using one of your dumb metaphors! And another one, I might add that makes no sense—who cares if cookies are soft or tough as long as they're tasty!

But it did start, slowly, slowly, to get better for all the kids being bullied at Jarvis Middle School, not just Zachary and Leo. And there were A LOT of kids! Mrs. Wells was stunned at how many students, boys and girls, came into her office to tell about their experiences of being bullied. She made notes of all of them, and as promised, never asked or recorded any names, unless the kids wanted more help with the matter.

In a few months she had dozens of documented bullying incidents from 7th, 8th and 9th graders, including more and more on-line with social networking. And when the school year ended, she and Mr. Meredith met twice a month over summer vacation, and even more by e-mail and phone, to adjust and fine-tune their Anti-Bully Policy for the next term.

Leo's birthday fell on the very last day of school, and Zachary found him the perfect gift: a T-shirt with these words written on it: 'English is weird. It can be understood through tough, thorough thought, though'.

Summer then went by very fast for us all at the Klossner house. Too fast.

Shortly after a ten-day camping holiday near Yosemite National Park (I got to go! I got to go!), Mr. Klossner took his wife and two kids to the Hollywood premier of a film he'd worked on as Story Editor (I did NOT get to go! I did NOT get to go!). Zach told me it was a lame story about teenagers stuck in a huge amusement park until one plucky girl discovered it was actually a mock-up in a massive airport hangar, and that only by climbing up and over the moving roller coaster —a couple of kids were mushed on the tracks, 'cool effect' Zach noted—did they discover that they were part of a large military experiment run by an evil scientist, and blah, blah, blah. (The 'blah, blah, blah' were Zach's exact words.)

Anyway, they got to meet the director and young stars and sit in the fourth row center with free popcorn.

Mrs. Klossner was only around sometimes as she'd taken a position teaching a summer extension course in Existentialism. Again, don't ask me what that is. You humans seem to like to make up crazy long words to sound important.

And THIS, Zach told me is the term for Fear of Long Words:

Hippopotomonstrosesquipedaliophobia.

Yeah, seriously.

Tristan kept on practicing her artwork all summer, and actually got so good that a few of her portraits— one was of me, please note—were accepted at a local Art Fair where she sold three and made $75! That's a lot of new pastels and paints and canvases! She even found an old easel on-line, and said she'd do a huge watercolor portrait of me next. HUGE! MOI!!

She started eleventh grade the second week in September, and Zach started ninth a few days later, back at Jarvis Middle School with longer hair and about two inches taller.

There was no sign of Joe Padilla, and when he asked Mrs. Wells about it, she said that they'd relocated over the summer to another town further up the coast, no reasons given.

Zachary said that he actually felt bad for Joe. Not that they ever became friends. In fact, the best we can say is that They Tolerated Each Other. But, hey, that's a whole lot better than being trapped in a locker or name-calling or bruises or hiding among trees to eat your lunch with pigeons pooping overhead!

One day in late September, Zachary arrived home more joyous and content than he's been since he got the highest score in miniature golf at his eighth birthday party.

At the dinner table he told his parents why, and I heard every word, sitting under the table waiting for

Tristan's hand to come down with yam hunks in it for me (she hates yam.) And in case you have not yet noticed, I have Total Recall. So here's what happened that evening just like it's taking place now:

"Something incredible happened today in P.E.," Zach said after swallowing a mouthful of broccoli (which I'm glad he likes and doesn't offer under the table, as I find it detestable. Yes, a new word! I am listening to Zach when he looks up words he doesn't know, encouraged by Mrs. Wells.

Detestable: adjective; deserving of intense dislike. Yep, that's broccoli!)

"We're all ears, Zach," his father said, also secretly handing down hunks of yam without anybody noticing.

"On Tuesday we had to play tag football, you know, where instead of tackling you just have to yank fabric bits that are velcro-ed on a belt..."

"Huh??" Tris looked over to her brother like he just said 'zrishna koppal vloomy'.

Mr. Klossner turned to her and explained.

"Tackle football's too dangerous to attempt in P.E. class, Tris, so they play Tag Football. That's how we played in high school, too. The official games with the school teams are different. They tackle for real."

"Go on, Zach," Mrs. Klossner said (NOT handing me hunks of yam, darn it!).

"So, like suddenly, I got through the defensive line 'cuz I'm thin and all, and I actually grabbed the flags off the quarterback!"

"The WHAT?" Tris asked.

"The one who throws the ball at the beginning," Mr. Klossner told her.

"Oh… ," Tris mumbled as she snuck a large chunk of yam—buttered!—under the table for Moi.

"So anyways," Zach continued, "I managed to do it again, get the flags off. Then again! And suddenly the other team captain is putting two, then three, then FOUR guys on me to stop me getting through, and I still slipped through and got the flags. When the game was over, our captain came over and pat me on the back!"

"Honey, that's great!" Mrs. Klossner said, dropping crumbs accidently when she ripped a piece of garlic bread in two, which all land right at my paws and are gobbled up in a second.

"So today, the captain picked me third to be on his team! THIRD!" he said putting down his fork. "And, okay, I'm not stupid. I know it's only to play offensive and slip through and get the flags, but I did it two more times today, and more and more kids pat me on the back and congratulated me."

His parents smiled at him, and in the distraction Tris slipped a HUGE hunk of yam down to me.

" I, Zachary Bartholomew Klossner, was picked third to be on a team in P.E.!'"

Okay, he didn't say that last line. I added it. He hates his middle name, remember?

But I thought that story needed a last line.

And so here are the last lines to THIS story:

I, Cassandra Cuddles Jasmine Beckett Bobolina, feel I am finally in a family where nothing is going to get me kicked out or lost. I have successfully moved up from the laundry room to the warm beds of the kids with quilts and pillows (goose down!), and okay, so every one of them doesn't feed me under the table (Yet!), but enough of my new family does. And though I think about my past and the other people who made me part of their family—some not so nice like the Heffernans, and some super nice like the Godots —I am HERE, and now part of the Klossner family.

No more being bullied, no more being abandoned or lost.

Let's see what my future brings.

I'm thinking DOG SHOW. But you silly humans don't show mongrels.

What we dogs call a Unique Blend.

That's me.

❖

THE END

PS—Oops, I almost forgot. I've been working all week on my own Limerick, and share it with you now.

I came back as a dog by choice,
to help a young boy find his voice,
and to rise up while seeing
the great worth of his Being,
and that's why we're called Man's Best Friend!

Okay, I admit I had trouble finding a third rhyme for choice/voice. But, hey, the integrity is there!
Integrity, noun; the quality of being Honest.

❖

THE END AGAIN

If you or anybody you know is being bullied at school, the first step is to inform somebody there—a teacher or administrator. The second is to realize that the

Bullying Is Not About Who You Are

but is about the bully's own problems which he/she is trying to take out on you. Ignoring them is much more powerful than attacking back. And Trust Me: It does stop eventually. Kids mature (even bullies) and it does NOT last forever!

For extensive advice on all forms of bullying, including cyber, there are many websites to explore, among them:

www.kidshealth.org

www.kidpower.org

www.kidscape.org.uk

www.standagainstviolence.co.uk

www.mayoclinic.org

And in the USA call toll-free:

Stopbullying Lifeline 1-800-273-8255

In the UK call toll-free:

ChildLine 0800-1111

AUTHOR'S NOTE

Some of what happened to Zachary I wrote from my own Middle School experiences growing up in San Jose, California (though we called it junior high).

My older brother, I later learned, had it much worse than me, the bullying going on well into his college years.

The mild bullying I experienced formed much of my identity from age 13-15, when it finally subsided as I stumbled upon a valued role in the all-important testing ground of school Sports. (Yes, being slim allowed me to slip through the Defense in tag-football and grab the flags, just like Zachary.) Also, as Zachary's sister says, it does get much better in high school when kids mature out of their gawky struggle with prepubescence.

I do believe, though that the best policy towards any aggression is to defuse it by not playing into it, as many wise humans over the centuries have suggested ('Turn the other cheek'). Sadly, the leaders and institutions in our Western Culture follow none of their wise advice, and always react to political violence with bigger, badder, bolder violence. And most of us individuals take our cues from that. Thus we have the current state of affairs, both internationally and domestically. And personally.

But as the Dali Lama says (Tristan should have this tacked on her wall!):

'Instead of getting angry, nurture a deep caring and respect for troublemakers, because by creating such trying circumstances they provide us with invaluable opportunities to practice tolerance and patience'.

And:

'We can let the circumstances of our lives harden us so that we become increasingly resentful and afraid, or we can let them soften us and make us kinder. You always have the choice.'

ACKNOWLEDGEMENTS

Alison Leslie Gold, *First, for being a dear and loyal friend for two decades now. A couple years ago she asked me to collaborate with her on a book she was working on for Middle Grade, which eventually became 'Elephant in the Living Room'. She then generously gave me permission to continue with the dog-witnesses-family-issues story, which resulted in the book before you now*

Jakob Urban & Felizitas Fischer, *who invited me to stay up at their Himalayan paradise in India (along with their six dogs. Six!) where the first draft of this book was written*

Kimberly Roseth & Joy Strayer & Lauren Levian, *for their kind and helpful editing*

Lorcan La Plante and Siena Barr of UK, *young adults, for their input and comments.*

Hanaan Rosenthal, *for his consideration and patience in seeing this through to publication.*

Lastly,
I want to give thanks to the two people who befriended me the most through childhood,

Leo Taiariol, *who was my best friend (and next door neighbor) from age 2-12*

Rob Wyman, *a friend onward through high school, co-creator of fake vomit and the kid trapped in the locker by bullies.*

And again
our great family dog Samuel Jacob Moses, who first taught me love & respect for pets.

www.ingramcontent.com/pod-product-compliance
Lightning Source LLC
Chambersburg PA
CBHW060154070426
42447CB00033B/1312